The Fast And Easy

7 Steps To Becoming A Network Marketing Professional For Business

Jack Connor

This book is dedicated to the Network Marketing Distributor.

Thank you for having the courage to follow your dreams.

Contents

Introduction

I remember the day I was first introduced to Network Marketing. It was January 1998. I was 23 years old and I was selling real estate for a small company owned by my father and his friend J. Joyce.

I had just gotten married and had a little son. I was already behind in paying my bills, and I was scared. The year before, he had made $ 45,000 in commissions from real estate sales, which was very good. The problem was that I had spent $ 60,000 and had not saved money to pay my taxes, which had to be covered in a few months.

When J. Joyce came to my desk that day and said, "Eric, I think I have a way for us to make some extra money," I said, "Tell me more!" He said that a good friend of his had something to show us and invited us to his house. So I got in the car with my dad and John and we went to see him.

When we arrived, he took us into his living room, put a tape in his VCR, and pressed PLAY. I sat down and watched this crazy video. It was filled with mansions, limos, and statements from people making fortunes almost overnight. It was so exaggerated that I couldn't believe it was true, so I told them that it seemed like a bad idea and that I wasn't interested. My natural mental filters couldn't let it in.

Then something happened. John and my dad said, "Ok, too bad. We are going to do it ".

This had a BIG impact on me, as the only thing worse than being broke and in debt was thinking that these two would make a lot of money without me! So I changed my attitude, pulled my dad aside, and asked him if he would lend me some money so I could register. Thank God he said yes because deciding to become a Network Marketing distributor changed my life.

When I started, I treated this business like most people, that is, I did not treat it like a business. He walked in, made a few calls, and hoped he was lucky enough to make some money. And at first it worked! DO make money and it was very exciting, I have to say something though. During those first few months, my whole strategy was to quickly call all of my dad's contacts before he could. I thought that if I called them, I would tell them that my dad and J. Joyce were also part of this, and I would get a meeting with them or for them to see a video, and if they were interested later, my father would not fight over who did it because I it was in their organization. I had limited success with this but, as you can imagine, it didn't last long.

And so, three months after starting, my Network Marketing income ended. And when it happened, my positive attitude disappeared. I began to blame everyone and everything for my lack of success. My contact was not helping me enough. The company did not provide adequate training. I didn't know enough people. Nobody respected me for being young. He blamed the product. He blamed the company. He blamed the economy. I blamed everyone but myself.

But he had a big problem. Blaming the world wasn't helping to pay my bills. And I had quit real estate sales after my first commission check. It was going to take a long time to get a real commission on a real estate sale, and I didn't have a college degree, so getting a decent job wasn't an option. The only place where I could get any money was in Network Marketing.

So I put my head down and went to work. At first it was not easy. In fact, in my first three years I rebuilt my organization seven times! He managed to pick it up and it would fall to pieces, and he would pick it up again and it would fall again. And again.

After those three years, I was very discouraged. He had almost given up hope. Then something happened that changed my life. In fact it was a combination of two things. It was the night before the company convention and I was watching a news program on television. They had a guest who was an expert on a subject that I don't remember well. What crossed my mind at that moment was: "How does someone become an expert on THAT subject?" The only thing I could think of is that they must have decided to get experience, learn everything they could, read every book, talk to every person, and learn it completely in order to become an expert.

The next day I went to the company convention and watched one superstar after another as they walked across the stage. So, it was like being struck by lightning. At last my brain understood that if I really decided to do so, I could become a Network Marketing expert. I could focus on skills. I could practice until I became an expert, and NO ONE could stop me.

Until then, I was always looking for a focus. I was hoping to be lucky. I was hoping to find that superstar who was going to change everything. And I was afraid of losing my chance if that didn't happen soon.

In an instant, everything changed. I realized that I didn't have to worry about being lucky. The position and timing were a good thing, but they weren't necessary for long-term success. I didn't have to worry about my advisor, meeting the right person, or anything else. All I had to do was become an expert.

So I decided that on that day I would change my focus and develop the skills to become a Network Marketing Professional. That was the day that changed my life.

Since then, my life has been an amazing adventure. Network Marketing became a career for me. I have complete freedom over my time. I have met the most amazing people all over the world. I have been able to touch and be touched by the lives of hundreds of thousands of people, I have traveled the world, I have contributed to the causes that are important to me, and most of all, I have become a better person in the process.

All of this happened for me and it can happen for you too. In this book, I am going to give you the fundamental principles that can guide you to become a Network Marketing Professional. They have been very useful to me over the last few decades and I know they will be very useful to you too.

Welcome to an exciting adventure!

CHAPTER 1

Network Marketing Isn't Perfect ... It's Just Better

Are you feeling restless? Are you dissatisfied? Do you feel that there must be a better way of doing things in terms of your job and the way you earn a living?

The good news: YES there is a better way, but it is different than what you were taught in school. Let me explain.

When I travel and speak around the world, I like to play a game with audience participation. I ask people to help me create the best business possible and ask them to mention specific things that they would like to have in that business, as well as things to avoid. I always get an interesting list. If we were face to face, I would do the same with you. But since that's not the case, let's summarize what people in over 30 countries have told me as I create what I like to call "The Perfect Profession List."

People usually start by naming what they don't want:

- No boss

- Without commuting to work

- No alarm clock

- No employees

- No policies

- No compromises

- Without discrimination

- No educational requirements

Later, as people use their imaginations in a more positive way, they begin to visualize the positive characteristics:

- Something positive

- Great product or service

- Unlimited income

- Residual income

- Enjoy the people you work with

- Time freedom

- Something significant

Network Marketing Isn't Perfect ... It's Just BETTER

- Personal growth

- Lots of benefits

- International

- Contribute to laudable causes

- Low risk

- Low startup costs

- Economy resistant • Fiscal benefits

- Fun!

Now you could add some attributes, but don't you agree that it's a very good start? Imagine being able to enjoy a profession with all those attributes!

16

All the "jobs" that I know of fall into one of five categories:

- Blue collar

- White collar

- Sales

- Owner of a traditional business

- Investments

Blue Collar Professions

This is the definition of blue collar on Wikipedia. "A blue collar worker is a member of a working class who does manual labor." My definition is someone who works to fix something, make something, clean something, build something, or service something (or someone).

In my life, I have had many blue collar professions. And, for those who have been in this line of work, there is a certain satisfaction for a job well done.

But here's the big question: Can a blue-collar worker meet the Perfect Profession List? The obvious answer is no. Sure, it can meet some of the attributes. You can have a great product and low start-up costs or with some of the other items on the list, but if you really watch, the blue collar worker can't get you where you want to be. It doesn't take you to "The Perfect Profession." White Collar Professions

This is the definition of white collar on Wikipedia.

"The term white-collar worker refers to the person who performs professional, administrative or administrative work, in contrast to a blue-collar worker, whose job requires manual labor. White collar work usually takes place in an office or cubicle. "

My definition is a person who is employed by someone else to perform activities other than manual labor or sales.

Many people choose a white collar profession, as it is one of the most accepted options available by society. It has long been established as the safe and reliable option. Recently, that has changed. The implicit contract that if you are loyal to the company the company will be loyal to you is long gone.

I have also been a white collar worker. In my experience, there are two types of people who do this type of work: High achievers and Hideouts.

Achievers are people who want to perform at the highest level possible. They are ambitious, motivated and energetic. They are full of ideas and want to climb the corporate ladder, which are great attributes to have. But there is a downside to the Achiever.

As soon as a person decides to become an Achiever, they also become a target. Your boss sees you as a threat to their job, so they either start to do less or attack your reputation. His colleagues see him as a person who will either leave them to shame or prevent them from getting a promotion, so he begins to do everything they can to undermine his achievements.

So, to remain an Achiever and to survive in this hostile environment, a person must become very good at something that has nothing to do with their productivity - and that is in politics. They must learn to navigate the political world by reducing their enemies and strengthening their relationships with powerful people. In fact, some of the most successful people in the corporate world are not

Achievers. They are pure politicians.

So if you decide to work in the corporate world and you have to be an Achiever, you have to accept the fact that you also have to be a good politician.

Now, let's talk about the Hideouts. These are the people who HATE politics, but still need a job. These people learn not to be ambitious Achievers. They do not stick out. They do not speak in meetings.

They do not bring new ideas. They hide. They keep their heads down and do what they are told to do. They do only enough so that they are not talked about in a negative way. They survive.

And this has worked for decades. But in the New Economy, hiding is increasingly difficult. And people are running out of time.

Okay, let's go back to our Perfect Profession Checklist: Can a white-collar worker fulfill the list? Again, the answer is clear: no - certainly not in many areas. Sales

Some people choose to walk away from being an "employee" and start a career in sales. This is certainly more intrepid as salespeople are usually paid on the basis of their production and not by the hour.

I have met thousands of salespeople. There is a common theme that I have observed over the course of my career. The typical salesperson will have a period in which everything works out perfectly. Everything they touch turns to gold and they earn some very good money.

As soon as that happens, they almost always establish a lifestyle suitable for that income level. They buy a new house, they buy new cars, they enroll their children in better schools, they buy a vacation home - they buy it all. Everything is fine for a while.

And then something changes. The company changes the compensation plan, its territory is reduced, a competitor appears, they lose their best customer, the economy goes into recession, a new technology makes their offering less valuable, or government regulations for their industry change. These are just a few examples. There are hundreds of reasons why the world of a salesperson can be (and probably will be) more complicated.

When that happens, coupled with the great lifestyle they have developed, 40 hours a week is not enough to pay the bills. So they go up to 50 hours per week. And then to 60. And then to 70. And then his life is very small. Yes, they have many things, but they don't have time to enjoy them.

The other challenge for the sales profession, no matter how a person performs, is that they will have to start from scratch the next day. It can be very tiring to live under this kind of pressure for a long period of time.

Can the sales profession pay the bills? Sure. Can you fulfill The Perfect Profession we've described earlier? Again, the answer is no.

Owner of a Traditional Business

Some people go for the big dream - to build their own business where they are the boss and make all the decisions. It's an exciting idea, right? This is the reality for most people:

Step one: They use their savings, take on new debt, and often borrow money from friends and family to get started.

Step two: They incur more debt in the form of income and personal guarantees everywhere.

Step three: Now instead of focusing on what they're good at (let's say they're good at sales and decide to start their own business), they have to be everything to everyone. They act as an attorney for legal matters, an accountant for financial matters, and a collection agent for accounts receivable. They even take out the trash. They do EVERYTHING except sell, being that's what they're good at.

Step four: They battle. Instead of owning your own business, the business owns them. They are the first person to come to work and the last to leave. And after everyone else gets paid, they can possibly get enough money to at least pay their own bills, but that doesn't allow you to reduce the debt incurred to start your own business.

Step five: They succeed or fail. They either come to a point along the way where their business succeeds or they fail, often filing for bankruptcy and taking a job in sales or a corporate setting again. And even if they do succeed in their business, that usually means a life filled with long hours of work and stress.

Sounds romantic right? If you've never started your own business, ask your friends if they have about whether or not this description is appropriate. Most people who start their own business don't mind getting a return on their investment. They just want to get their investment BACK. It is very clear that owning a traditional business cannot meet the Perfect Profession List that we have outlined. Investor

The last category for the ways you can earn a living today is that of the investor. What do you need to be an investor? Money, right? If you do not have a lot of money, it will be very difficult to make a living from the returns on your investments, especially if you try to be conservative to reduce the risk of loss.

But let's say you do. What is the second thing you need to be a successful investor? You need to be very skilled and have a lot of knowledge. I can talk about those who have been skilled real estate investors. But when things changed dramatically in the real estate market, their skills couldn't help them. They lost big.

Would you like to invest in someone's traditional business? Good luck. In most cases, you will not be able to be an investor; you will end up being a philanthropist.

And how about the stock market? People don't do so well there, do they? A few people do well, at least once in a while. But I know people who have lost and then won, especially in the last decade. It's hard to get a guaranteed return when you're not in control. And trust me, as investors you are NOT in control. Anything can happen, overnight.

Let me tell you a story to illustrate this point. At the end of 2001, I was living large. I had just sold a company that I co-founded and was working as a highly paid consultant. For my share of the sale, I received approximately 170,000 shares in the new company. The company was listed on the New York Stock Exchange and the price was around $ 44 per share, which meant that my stock was worth around $ 7.5 million. I had a great income and a great investment portfolio. My life was the BEST.

I used part of my shares to obtain a loan to build a house for about $ 2 million dollars, for the house of my dreams that I was going to build. As for the rest, I did not diversify because I knew that the company was in excellent condition with a good product and a phenomenal sales team.

Then something happened out of my control. Overnight the stock traded to $ 37 a share by a group of investors who had focused on the company and shorted their shares. In itself, the lower the share price fell, the more money they would make.

I thought it was ridiculous because the company was doing very well, so I bought more shares at $ 37 dollars, using my current shares as collateral, knowing that the price would go up. It went down to $ 33. I bought more shares. It went down to $ 27. I started getting warnings about margin calls, which meant that if I didn't send them money, they were going to start selling my shares to cover the losses. I had no money to send.

Shares continued to decline. They were down to $ 10 a share and my $ 7.5 million was gone. Poof! All in less than 90 days. Eventually, the stock rose in price and the company was privatized at $ 65 per share. But I wasn't there to capitalize on that situation. It was finished.

Could I have been smarter? Sure. Did I make mistakes? Absolutely. But here's the lesson: If you're going to be an investor, you have to accept that from time-to-time things will get out of your control. And when that happens, it can be very expensive.

Well, let's go back to the Perfect Profession List.

Can being an investor, something put to meet the list? I do not believe it.

We've talked about blue collar work, white collar work, sales, owning a traditional business, and being an investor. And none of those activities can meet our Perfect Profession List. Is it even possible to have the perfect profession? The answer is yes, but to get there you need to understand that everything is changing. The old models of compensation are dead or dying, and we are going through the greatest economic change of all our lives.

The NEW Economy

The world as you know it has changed. For those who do not recognize this fact, it will be the worst of times. For those who do, it will be the best of times.

During the last 100 years, an interesting phenomenon has occurred. The rise of the corporation became the standard in society. The safe and respected place for people to exist in a workplace was being an employee.

Step one: Go to a school to learn how to be an employee.

Step two: Find a company that hires you.

Step three: He works for that company for 40 years.

Step four: Retire.

In recent decades, the promise of being rewarded by the company for your loyalty and hard work has been exposed as a myth. People began to realize that the loyalty they were giving to their company was not being returned to them. So, a different process evolved.

Step one: Go to a school to learn how to be an employee.

Step two: Find a company that hires you.

Step three: Change companies for various political and economic reasons, every three to five years, during the course of your career.

Step four: Realize that you can't retire comfortably after 40 years, so you keep working.

And now we are going through the biggest change of all our lives. For a century, companies have paid their employees by the hour, by the week, or by the year. This is changing globally.

The world is moving toward a performance-based economy. And it is already happening. Here's what that means: In the future, you will only get paid based on your performance. They won't pay you for your time. People in the food service industry already live by this model. They get low hourly pay, as required by law, and they earn their money based on tips that are based on their performance.

If you can imagine that the same model is applied in practically every job in the world, you will realize that it is on the way. The person who cleans the rooms in a hotel will not be paid by the hour, they will be paid by the room.

For office workers, here is an example.

A person has an annual salary of $ 60,000 dollars.

Step one: The company will reduce his salary to about $ 50,000 because in today's market there are people who take a job for a lesser amount.

Step two: They will reduce your "base" salary to something around $ 20,000.

Step three: They will tell that person that they can earn an additional $ 30,000 during the year if they meet certain performance goals on a monthly basis.

In other words, if you meet your goals, you can earn an additional $ 2,500 per month. Now there is great pressure, and the company loves it. If you don't meet the statistic targets, they can save even more money. If you MEET the goals, guess what your future is? Requirements are going to increase.

Unless you are extremely specialized, this will happen to you, if it hasn't happened already. You can bet on it. And that will happen for every profession worldwide. The evolution has begun.

Why has this happened? First, for being a better model for the company. They will get better results thanks to better costs. Second, the New Economy needs fewer people, so companies have fewer people competing for fewer and fewer jobs.

Let me explain why the New Economy needs fewer people. The exponential increase in technology has changed everything. For the last 100 years,

90% of the population worked in agriculture. Today, due to dramatic increases in efficiency, it is less than 1%, and farm jobs have disappeared.

Remember the customer service call centers where you talked to people? Today, you talk to a machine, and those jobs have disappeared. Remember when companies had a lot of salespeople? Today people shop online, and those jobs have disappeared. Do you remember Blockbuster Video and all of its employees? Today people watch movies on their mobile devices and tablets, and those jobs have disappeared. I love books, and you should go to your local bookstore while you still can. Soon they will be history, and the jobs that those stores have will also disappear.

I could go on and on with practically every category of job in the world. Technology and efficiency are eliminating jobs every day and there is nothing we can do to stop it. In fact, it will only continue to accelerate. If you're sitting around waiting for the economy to pick up and jobs to come back, stop. They will not return.

Just as farmers' children saw the signs and left the farm to find new vocations, the same is happening for people in Old Economy jobs. To survive, they will need to open their eyes to this reality and find something new.

Network Marketing is BETTER

The best way I know not only to survive, but to excel in the New Economy, is Network Marketing. There are important products and services today, all over the world, that need to be promoted to the people who need them. Consumers still need to be educated.

Companies have options. They can enter the increasingly fragmented world of advertising to spread the word, they can hire a large and expensive sales team to sell their products or services, or they can use Network Marketing to tell their story to the world. .

More and more companies will choose to use Network Marketing as it fits in with the New Economy. They can provide full corporate support and pay all distributors simply based on their performance in promoting their products. It is extremely efficient because, in the New Economy, word of mouth is still the best way to promote a product or service. The company can use the money they would have spent on advertising and promotion and pay their distributors out of it to spread the word.

What that means to you as an entrepreneur is that you can receive all the benefits of owning a traditional business, but without the typical risks of it. And there will be no cap on your income because Network Marketing companies WANT you to earn all the money you can earn. If you're going to get paid based on your performance anyway, why set a cap?

The "Detail" of Network Marketing

This all sounds great, and it is. But there is a detail that most people do not mention. Here it is:

You must accept a temporary loss of your social esteem for ignorant people.

This means that, for a time, people who are still living and trying to function in the old system will think less of you. They will not understand. They will think you are crazy for being involved in Network Marketing.

In fact, the word "accept" is not completely accurate. You need to do more than that. You need to embrace the temporary loss of your social esteem for ignorant people. YOU are seeing the future before it becomes apparent to others. YOU are the smart one. YOU are the person who is acting to live a better life.

There are a reason people will think of you that way, and it's not just because you're stuck in the old system. Let's see if I can make you understand all this better, because if you decide that Network Marketing is your profession, it is important that you know it.

Most people have either joined a Network Marketing company or know someone who has. This is what goes through the minds of almost everyone who decides to get involved. "Hmm, I can think of five or six people who do this! My sister would be great for this! My friend loves this kind of thing. I know another great person for this! Ok, I'm going to do it. "

In other words, they are not joining the profession. They're just hoping to get lucky, get a few people to join the project to cover their own startup costs, and sit around waiting for the money to start coming in. The attraction of getting paid for someone else's effort is powerful but is often misunderstood.

They have not started a real business. They have simply bought a glorified lottery ticket. Imagine a lottery ticket with six chances to scratch and win. Those opportunities represent each of the people the new person thinks will surely join. They reach out to those people and try to get them to bond. Due to their lack of skill, most end up with nothing - just like a lottery ticket. This becomes just another missed opportunity, and because they have acted ignorantly and without any skill, they have possibly damaged some friendships as well.

So they tear up the ticket instead of taking responsibility for not starting a real business and blaming Network Marketing, making sure to tell everyone: "Look, I've been there. I have done. I have talked to everyone I know, and Network Marketing is not working. Save your money ".

THAT is what you will face if you choose this as your profession - the opinion of ignorant people who think they have done it correctly, and that it does not work. If that's going to be too much for you, then Network Marketing is not for you. But if you can accept it, the world is yours.

People who accept it get A LOT of money. Companies pay unlimited amounts to people who can help the blind to see, who educate the ignorant, and who can build a community of like-minded people.

Some people like to say, "Perception is Reality." I really hate that saying. All the great leaders of the world have ignored it for centuries. What if Nelson Mandela had said that perception is reality? What if Martin Luther King Jr. had said that perception is reality? What if Steve Jobs had said that perception is reality? The great leaders of the world said: "Reality is reality and I am going to do everything I can to help people understand it."

The truth is that Network Marketing is not perfect. It's just BETTER. And that is the reality!

CHAPTER 2

If you are going to be part of network marketing, Decide to be a professional. Decide on Go Pro

There are three categories of people in Network Marketing. I have seen them all and I have been all. They are the Imposters, the Amateurs and the Professionals. Impostors

Imposters treat this profession like a lottery ticket. They are hoping they can earn a lot with as little effort as possible. When I started, I was an Impostor, hoping to win thanks to the work of my father and his partner. Luckily, I got some results and that allowed me to move on, at least in the short term. But I think you will agree with me that staying an Imposter is a bad idea. Within 90 days I had left that category and became an Amateur. Amateurs

Amateurs focus on different things. One of the things I continued to focus on as an amateur was luck. I really hoped to get lucky and sign a great distributor who was going to make me rich. We have all heard the stories about a person whose life was changed by a record. In reality, even if some of those stories are true, it doesn't help our profession much because it makes people spend their time waiting for that one great moment.

The second thing I focused on as an amateur was timing. I always worried about the right moment. Did I get there early enough? Could you be the youngest person at the highest level in the company? How many other leaders were there already in the local market? Were there already many against whom to compete? Were there enough to jumpstart things? Was it too big? Did I miss the growth curve? Was it too small? He was obsessed with the timing.

The third thing I focused on as an amateur was position-wise. Was he in the correct organization? Were there other people in a better position than mine? Maybe he didn't have the right contact. Would I be better off elsewhere?

And the fourth thing I was focusing on as an amateur was shortcuts. I was always looking for a new angle.

Whatever trick he found, he used it. Newspaper advertising? Okay. Help wanted signs posted on the side of the roads. Let's do it. Deliver flyers at the mall? Sure. Go door to door? Let's try it. The Internet did not exist when I was an Amateur. Imagine how insanely crazy and happy he would be with all the tactics of

Internet that I could have used and that would have distracted me. What I mean is that every time I heard about a new approach being taught by someone in the world, I was looking for a shortcut to it.

Then, in the end, I decided on Go Pro (being a Professional). Wikipedia's definition for a professional is: "A person who is paid to perform specialized tasks and complete them in exchange for a fee."

My definition of a Network Marketing Professional is: "A person who is an expert in the skills necessary to build a large and successful Network Marketing organization."

There is a phrase in our profession that does more harm than good. It says: "Ignorance on fire is better than frozen knowledge." The point of this phrase is that it is better to be excited and ignorant than listless and intelligent. That may be true, but why choose one or the other?

Let me give you an example. Let's say you need an operation. In the hospital, you meet your doctor. He comes in and says, "I'm very excited to have your operation done. I am so passionate about it that I can hardly sleep. Nobody on the planet wants to help you more than me. " You say, "Wow, thank you doctor. How long have you been carrying out this type of operation? ". He replies, "Well, I've never actually studied for this particular operation. I have never practiced it and I have never done it, but that does not matter because I am very passionate about this! ". How are you going to feel?

Enthusiasm is good, but eventually you need to match passion with skills.

Professional athletes spend hours and hours preparing for a competition, but when it comes to joining Network Marketing, they don't spend a day learning our skills. Doctors dedicate decades of their lives, with very high expenses, to be better doctors, but when it comes to joining Network Marketing, they do not spend a month studying and practicing being a Professional.

In his book Outliers, Malcolm Gladwell's research showed that it takes approximately 10,000 hours of practice to get to an expert level at something. With four hours of practice a day, this brings us to a total of about seven years. That formula also applies to Network Marketing. It will take about seven years to be world class. The good news is that this profession is a bit more flexible, and you can earn a lot of money while becoming an expert. The trick is not being satisfied with it. Don't stop learning even when you are making money.

When I decided to go Pro (go pro), everything changed for me. I stopped focusing on luck, at the right time, position and shortcuts. I even stopped focusing on money.

My world changed when I started to focus on skills and made a commitment to practice, practice, and practice until I mastered it.

Another thing that happened when I decided on Go Pro. Suddenly, my group started to grow. It was as if people could feel my shift in focus and commitment to excellence and wanted to be a part of it. Think about a time in your life when you were close to a person with a commitment to excellence. It may have been a teacher, a coach, a boss, or a friend. How did it make you feel? It inspired you, right? You will find that you will inspire others when you make this important change.

If you are going to be part of this great profession, decide to do it well and treat it as a profession. If you go for Go Pro, this business is great. If you keep yourself as an Impostor or Amateur, you are going to be miserable.

Now you have noticed that I use the word profession a lot. I do it on purpose. Network Marketing is more than just a project. It is not an industry; it is a profession. If you, do it right, it's a great race. It can cause you to leave work in a job that does not make you happy, to reach a state of complete freedom.

That's why I called my site NetworkMarketingPro.com. This is what I say to people every day: "Ladies and gentlemen, my wish for you is that you decide to become Network Marketing Professionals - that you decide to Go Pro, for it is a fact that we have a better way. Now let's tell the world".

When the site launched on March 11, 2009, very few people called themselves Network Marketing Professionals. That is no longer the case. Millions of people have changed the way they think about our business and I am proud of it.

*•	I look forward to the day when it is common for people to hear:*

*•	I am a doctor, but I am also a Network Marketing Professional.*

*•	I work in construction, but I am also a Network Marketing Professional.*

*•	I am an athlete, but I am also a Network Marketing Professional.*

The more people hear these words, the more the world will be ready for a better way.

CHAPTER 3

As In Any Profession, You Will Need To Learn Some Skills

I hope you have already convinced yourself that Network Marketing is a better way. I hope I have also made it clear that if you are going to be a part of it, it is better to become a professional. The next step is to recognize that you need to learn some skills. But before we review those skills, let me give you some good news.

Unlike most professions, you won't need a lot of money for your education. You won't need to get a student loan, and you can even earn money while you learn. Also, this profession is not judgmental. In fact, it is the fairest opportunity in the entire world. Your background, experience, contacts, age, race or gender will not be factors in your ability to learn the skills that will allow you to decide on Go Pro.

Also, this is not complicated. The skills necessary for a business to be large and successful are easy to learn and you will be amazed at the number of people who will help you learn.

There are three basic elements for your Network Marketing business.

1)   First, you have the company's products. If some people are successful in advertising those products and you are not, it is not the fault of the product. In other words, everyone in the company has the same product to offer.

2)   Second, you have the company's compensation plan. If some people make a lot of money and you don't, it's not the compensation plan's fault. There is no plan for men and one for women. There is no plan for different age groups, or by educational background, or by skin color.

The plan is the same for everyone.

3)   The third element is the most important, and that is YOU. You are the only variable. They all have the same product and compensation plan, but you will be the difference between success and failure.

That means that at this point, you need to fully accept responsibility for your Network Marketing business. Decide today that you will never blame anyone or anything for your lack of results.

In fact, in Network Marketing there is something like an epidemic. People love to blame their contacts (the people above them in the structure) for all their problems. "If my contact did this or that for me, everything would be better."

If you are committed to building a large and successful organization, I want to advise you to do something important. I want you to say goodbye to your contact. Call them and tell them something like:

"I want to thank you for this opportunity. I appreciate. Having your own business is important and I appreciate you introducing me to the company you believe in and in which I now believe. But from now on, when it comes to building my business, I will use you as a resource and not as an excuse. Possibly call you from time to time. If you are available, that's great. If you're not, this is fine too. I am going to build my business and I understand one thing: This begins and ends with me ".

Everything changes when you accept full responsibility for your Network Marketing career.

Would it surprise you to know that there are only seven fundamental skills necessary to build a great business in Network Marketing? Seven, not 70. Each one is very basic, but it always amazes me how little effort people make to learn them. If a course on Network Marketing were offered in college, it would be one of the easiest classes to take. It's not rocket science, but you'll be glad to know that it's one of the highest paid skill sets in the world. Let's explore each one together.

CHAPTER 4

Skill # 1 — Find Prospects

When we see people in Network Marketing, one of the big questions is: "Do I know someone?" They believe that if they know someone, they can be very successful, and that if they don't know anyone, they won't stand a chance. It sounds logical, but it is not true.

As I mentioned in CHAPTER 2, there are three types of people in Network Marketing: imposters, amateurs, and professionals. When it comes to finding prospects, imposters make a mental list of three, four, or five people who they hope will join their business, and their entire future is based on the response of these people. If you are lucky enough to convince one of them, you can extend the life of your career for a short time. They can even make another mental list of three or four people. Eventually, or so we hope, they will decide to become amateurs.

Would it surprise you to know that roughly 80% of all people who join Network Marketing focus on building a business as imposters? It's true. The first approach of eight out of 10 distributors in this business is with the mentality of an imposter. They make a little mental list and see what happens. Your job is to make sure that you are not one of them and that you help your team avoid that. Educate people. Help them understand how powerful this opportunity can be if they treat it with due respect. For imposters, their only real chance is luck, and that luck must come quickly or they will fail.

The second group are the amateurs. Instead of making a little mental list, these people make a written list, which is a step in the right direction. Let's say you make a list of 100 prospects. They are launched with great enthusiasm but without much skill. They start with it and their list starts to shrink. As you get smaller and smaller, your anxiety level grows. His biggest fear is that there will be no more people to talk to. I know that was my biggest fear.

When I was in my early 20s, my list was nothing to brag about. As I mentioned, I tried to use my parents' contacts and it didn't take long for me to run out of names. Soon everyone knew what he was doing and had said yes or no. It was creepy. I felt that if I didn't find great people on my list, and if I didn't do it quickly, I was going to fail in this business.

It never occurred to me that finding quality people as prospects was a skill. Up to this point in my new profession, I always viewed "the list" as a ticket to wealth. If you had a good list, you would be successful, and if you had a bad one, you were either lucky or failed.

When I reached my defining moment and committed myself to becoming a professional, I began to study the people who had built large and successful organizations. I found that professionals treated finding people to talk to as one of their core skills. It was part of his job to find new people. They weren't interested in luck. They weren't worried about their list running out. They developed the skill to make sure that never happened. The professionals started with a written list. But afterward they vowed to never stop adding to the list. They created something called an "Active Candidate List," and I'm going to show you how to do the same.

One of the people who taught me how to do this right was Harvey Mackay, author of the bestselling How to Swim with the Sharks

Without Being Eaten Alive(How to Swim with Sharks Without Being Eaten Alive). Harvey is a good friend and is also one of the best in network marketing in the world. I once asked him how he built such a long list of influential friends. He told me that when he was 18 years old, his father sat down with him and said, "Harvey, from now on and for the rest of your life, I want you to take every person you meet, get their contact information, and find a creative way to stay in touch ". He has done that for more than 60 years, and today his friends list has more than 12,000 people. And they are not just social friends. They are true friends, and I consider myself lucky to be among them.

If you want to master this skill, follow these four easy steps:

Step one: Your list will be as complete as possible. Include everyone you can think of. ALL. It doesn't matter if they are a prospect or not. Your database will be one of your most important assets. They all go on the list. If they are negative, you put them on your list. If you hate them, put them on your list. If they are your best friend, put them on your list. If they've told you, "Never get into Network Marketing," put them on your list. If they are 98 years old, put them on your list. If they are 18 years old, put them on your list.

It is important to do so, because as you empty your mind towards paper, you will leave room for new contacts. When you write down your nephew, you will start to think about the circle of people around your nephew. All of these connections will become apparent as you work through your list. Think of everything - every organization you've been involved with, every group you've been a part of everything you've done. If you do it right, it will be hundreds and hundreds, or maybe thousands, of people.

Not all the people on your list need to be prospects. That decision is yours. But it is extremely important that you do the necessary work to put your network on paper.

Step two: Have you heard of the concept that we are all six contacts away from anyone in the world? Six degrees of separation? I don't know if it's a myth or if it's true, but I believe in the concept. Step two is looking at your list and thinking about the people you know - the second degree of separation. You probably know most of them.

Think of the members of your family. Who do you know? Add them to your list. Think about your friends. Who do you know? Add them to your list. Think of all the relationships in your life. Who do you know? Add them to your list. Don't worry about what you are going to do with that list. We will talk about that later. Just keep making it grow.

Step three: Expand your list constantly. That's why professionals call it an "Active Candidate List." It never stops growing. Professionals have a goal of adding at least two people to their list each day. They may not be prospects but, as Harvey Mackay's father said, they go on the list and you have to find creative ways to stay in touch. Harvey's book Dig Your Well Before Your Thirsty deals with this concept. If you think of this as a fundamental skill, you will realize that it is not very difficult. You come into contact with people every day. Just add them to your list. You meet people through social networks. Add them to your list. You do business with new people. Add them to your list.

My friend Jordan Adler is the author of Beach Money®, and he too has a seven-figure profit from Network Marketing. He is a master of step three. He lives his life and is always making new friends and if you look at his business, almost all the people he has recruited into his organization are people he did not know before starting his Network Marketing business. He is a professional.

Professionals develop a higher level of care. They pay attention to the world. They know they will meet new people all the time. Imposters and amateurs don't realize it. They just go through their day saying, "What people?

I don't see any person ".

How difficult would it be to increase your attention and add two new people each day? Think about it. If you, did it six days a week, it would be over 600 new people a year. Do it for 5 years, and there are more than 3,000 people. Can you see why professionals never worry about running out of people to talk to?

Please understand that I am NOT saying that you should jump on these people with your proposal the moment you meet them. Some people in Network Marketing make that mistake and it is not good. Just add them to the list, make friends, develop a connection, and when the time is right, you can help them understand what you have to offer.

Step four: Meet people on purpose. Professionals do it. It is difficult to meet new people if you are hiding from the world. Get out. Have fun. Sign up for a gym. Have a fun new hobby. Volunteer for a cause that is important to you. Find places and organizations where you can meet new people. Not only will it be good for your business, but you will also make great friends.

CHAPTER 5

Skill # 2 — Invite Prospects to Understand Your Product or Opportunity

Once you have identified your prospects, the next skill is to learn to properly invite them to learn more about your product or opportunity. This is by far the most important skill to develop. I call it the "entry" skill for Network Marketing. If you are unsuccessful in trying to get people to see what you have to offer, then we can guess what your future in MLM will be like.

Most people think that they should start with a great reputation and have a lot of influence over others to review what you offer. That is not true. When I started in 1988, I had neither reputation nor influence. As soon as I finished high school, I attended community college for a semester before I dropped out, and I had a total of 18 jobs - all before I was 23 years old. Do you think that I had the respect of my community? I had nothing. And being a person who made between $ 5-10 an hour, all my friends were in the same situation and could not help me. Most of them still lived with their parents.

But I was desperate. At first, I supplemented with numbers what I was lacking in terms of my ability. I called everyone I knew and presented my proposal. Some were registered. Most do not. I placed ads in the local newspaper. I presented my proposal to everyone who responded to the ad. With all that activity, some signed up. Most do not.

I tried everything. It was like a hunter looking for an elephant. I was going everywhere with a gun / opportunity in my hand, and I was shooting at everything that moved. I didn't care about relationships. All that mattered to me was getting a new recruit. My attitude was: "Some do. Some do not. Does matters? The following!".

But being a hunter, everyone around me felt like prey and started avoiding me. And that was not fun. Even worse was that the people who did join my business tried to do the same, failed and quit.

After three or four years of frustration, I reached my turning point and began studying successful people in MLM to see what they did. What I found surprised me. They were not hunters. They were like farmers. They built relationships. They built friendships.

They learned how to gain the trust of the people they knew and were very skilled at conveying what they believed in their products and opportunities. His goal was not to immediately recruit his prospects. Their initial goal was to educate their prospects on what they had to offer and then let those prospects decide if it was something they wanted to do.

This was a BIG change in strategy for me and I started to see things differently. I put myself in the prospects' shoes and thought about what would be attractive to me and what would put me on the defensive. I realized how the professionals were getting great results. Instead of acting like sharks, they were like trainers or consultants. They built relationships and then offered common sense solutions to people's problems. Who wouldn't like that?

The other thing I noticed with the professionals is that they weren't giving a "pitch" about their product or opportunity. Instead, when the time was right, they invited people to do one of two things, based on the prospect's individual situation.

The first thing they did was invite people to attend some kind of event, such as one-on-one or two-on-one meetings with another member of their team, a phone conversation between three people, a small group presentation at their home. , an online seminar, a meeting at a local hotel, or a company event or convention. Professionals understand that personal interaction is a key component when seeking to build trust and transfer what is believed, in order to try to connect with people as much as possible.

The second thing they did was invite people to review some kind of tool. I am a BIG believer in using tools to help educate the prospect. Tools take many forms. They are CDs, DVDs, magazines, brochures, websites, and online presentations. With some companies, you can even let people try the product and treat that as a tool.

There is no question that technology is constantly evolving, offering us more and more convenient ways to help educate prospects, but I have to add my personal opinion based on my experience. While technology allows us to bring quality information to people, quickly, there is nothing like a physical tool. In a world of bits and bytes, and in the world of Network Marketing where it is important to build trust, a physical tool makes it real.

Of the two methods used to help educate prospects, events are the most effective. There are many reasons. There is a physical interaction when meeting people, and that helps build trust. There is an important element of "social proof." It is valuable to the prospect to be able to see that there are other people actively involved, and to know what those people are like. There is education on the product and on the financial opportunity. They see the kind of support in person and realize that they won't have to do it all themselves. In most cases, there is excitement and urgency in these events. And they can listen to the stories of how other people are doing.

Those are some of the benefits. The only downside to events is that it can be difficult to schedule and confirm people, especially for a new person. If you do not have the necessary skills, it is very common to invite twenty people and only one or two show up. That can be daunting.

To build a large and growing organization, I have found a tool to be a better first step. Remember, your goal is education and understanding. We want people to know what we have and understand how it benefits their lives. A tool is a great way for people to educate themselves (and hopefully get excited), even with their busy lives. They may not have time to drive from one side of town to the other to get to know you, but they can listen to a CD in their car, watch a DVD, read a magazine, or watch a presentation online.

If you looked at my career you would see that, for me, the tools changed everything. In 1990 my company released a video that was dynamic and exciting. Although it was very expensive at $ 15 each back then it was worth it because when you learned to invite people to watch the video, the results were considerable.

Everyone in the company focused on a daily operating method focused on inviting people to watch our video. We did not allow distractions. Our entire culture went around this strategy and our growth went sky high. The events were important, but they were after getting one person to see the video.

By taking this new approach my organization finally exploded and I was able to enjoy the experience of having a group growing with or without me. It was very funny and difficult to describe. My group grew from a few dozen to a few hundred and then a few thousand. All I did was learn how to be successful inviting people to an event, teaching everyone to do the same.

The second major breakthrough in my career came with audiotape. Yes, I said audiotape. It was 1992 and it was all we had. The company was launching something new and exciting, and this time I personally recorded an audio that explained in detail the opportunity that presented itself. We sold each one for 50 cents, which covered our costs, and in less than a year, that little audiotape sold over a million copies. We taught people how to invite prospects to take that audiotape, put it in their car, and listen to it right away. The results were incredible.

We trained people to get 100 audiotapes first, they gave it to everyone they knew, and then they focused on getting two people a day. Using that simple system, my income grew to almost $ 1 million a year.

Different companies use various tools and events as strategies to grow their business. Some use house parties. Some use online presentations. Some use face-to-face meetings with magazines and charts.

Find what works best for your particular company, develop a daily method of operations, and then train people to do the same successfully and invite their prospects.

Like a pro, you are going to invite your prospects to review a tool or attend an event. Here's what you will NOT do: You will NOT present your proposal to people trying to amaze the world with your wisdom. That approach will feed your ego but rob your bank account.

Let me give you my formula for financial independence in Network Marketing.

Your ability to get a large group of people to consistently do a few simple things over an extended period of time.

It was this formula that helped me get out of the mediocrity in Network Marketing and will help you do the same.

For years, I focused on and depended on my ability to persuade people to join me. Then I graduated to find a few key leaders to train to do what I was doing. And finally, I learned the formula I just gave you and started focusing on getting a large group of people to consistently do a few simple things and continue to do them. When that happened, everything changed for the better.

Those are the basics. Let's take a moment to talk about the emotions of inviting. There are four basic rules.

Rule number one

You must emotionally detach yourself from the result. This is extremely important. Remember, our initial goal is education and understanding. We are not looking to get a new customer or sign up for a new distributor. In other words, if you separate your emotions from the result and focus solely on education and understanding, everything becomes simpler.

It sounds easy, but it really is difficult to do. We all enter this industry with the hope of recruiting very good people. It is difficult to disconnect from expectations. But you need to remember that we are not hunters. We are not sharking. Our job is to educate people and help them understand what we have to offer. We act as consultants offering suggestions on how people can live a better life.

If you focus on getting a new customer or distributor, you will constantly be disappointed and see your prospects turn away from you.

If you focus on education and understanding, you will have fun and your prospects will enjoy the experience.

Rule Number Two

Be yourself. Many people turn into someone else when they start inviting. This makes everyone uncomfortable. Be yourself. Focus on being the best.

Rule Number Three

Bring some passion. Enthusiasm is contagious. It's okay to get a little excited. Focus. Listen to some music that inspires you. Smile when you talk on the phone. I assure you that your positive emotions will translate into better results. Rule Number Four

Have a strong posture. This was a difficult thing for me. At first, I was insecure. I thought no one would take me seriously. But seeing the professionals, I realized their stance. They were bold. They had confidence in themselves. They were strong.

So, I decided it would be bold. I stopped apologizing all the time. Instead of saying, "Yes, I know I've had a lot of jobs in my life, but I hope this is the change I was looking for," I started to say, "Guess what? I am tired of the life I have led so far and I have decided to take action on the matter. I would not bet against me because I am serious ". Do you feel the difference?

Be yourself, but bolder. Be yourself, but stronger. Be yourself but have more confidence in yourself - at least you are inviting others. I realized that at first, I could do it for short periods of time, and just like when you start exercising a muscle, I could eventually do it for longer and longer, until it became part of me.

So now that we have everything prepared, let's review the formula for an invite. This formula has been designed to be used by phone or face to face. It should NOT be used by text message, email, or any other communication tool - only by phone or face-to-face. This can work with prospects from your known market (someone you know) or prospects from your unknown market (someone you know while living your life). I will give examples of both.

There are eight steps to a professional invitation. That may sound complicated, but with a little practice, you will find that it is an easy skill to master. Step One: You're in a hurry

Step Two: Praise the prospect Step Three: Make the invitation Step Four: If I do, will you?

Step Five: Confirmation # 1-Time Commitment

Step Six: Confirmation # 2-Confirm time commitment.

Step Seven: Confirmation # 3-Schedule the next call

Step Eight: Hanging

Step One: You're in a hurry

This is a psychological question. People are always attracted to someone else who has things to do. If you start each call or conversation face to face giving the impression that you are in a hurry, you will see that your invitations are short, with fewer questions, less resistance and people will respect you and your time more.

Examples for known market prospects:

"I don't have much time to talk, but it is always important to contact you."

"I have a million things to do, but I'm glad I found you."

"I'm on my way out, but I need to talk to you quickly."

Examples for unknown market prospects:

"Now is not the time to talk about this and I have to go, but ..."

"I have to go, but ..." "

You understand? Establish some urgency in your tone.

As for the examples I share with you, don't worry too much about the exact words. Focus on the concept and use your own words. Let people know that you are busy and that you have things to do and do not have much time, but that it is important for you to be able to talk to them quickly. And do it with some passion in your voice. Step Two: Praise the prospect

This is essential. A sincere compliment (and it should be sincere) opens the door to real communication and will make the prospect more accepting of hearing what you have to say.

Examples for known market prospects:

"You have been very successful, and I have always respected the way you do business."

"You have always supported me, and I really appreciate it very much" (Very good with family and close friends).

"You have an incredible mind for business, and you can see things that other people don't."

"For all the time I've known you, I've thought you are the best at doing what you do."

Examples for unknown market prospects:

"You have given me the best service I have ever received."

"You are very insightful. May I ask you to decide?

"You have made this a fantastic experience."

The key to praise is that it should be sincere. Find something you can honestly use to praise your prospect and use it. This simple step will literally double the results of your invitations. When you start with urgency and with a compliment, it will be very difficult for the person to react negatively to your invitation. People don't hear a compliment very often. It feels good. You will see that the prospects will be more receptive.

If you study the experts, you will see that they constantly put people in a good mood through their honest and sincere praise. They help to generate a good relationship, they help to open people's minds and, above all, they help us achieve our goal of education and understanding. Step Three: Make the Invitation

This is something where every situation is definitely different. There are three types of strategies when it comes to invitations from the Network Marketing Professional. The Direct Strategy

This is used when you invite people to learn more about an opportunity for THEM. Most people use a Direct Strategy for all of their prospects.

It usually goes like this: "I found a way for you to get rich! Let me tell you how. Bla bla bla".

I understand passion, but really, who's going to get excited about it unless I call them a millionaire?

That is not to say that the Direct Approach does not work. Works. It has an important place in the invitation process. But it should be reserved for people who know and respect you, or for people who you know are looking for something better.

Examples for known market prospects:

"When you told me that (you hate your job, you need more money, you want to find a new house, etc.), were you serious or were you just joking? (They almost always say they are serious). Well! I think I found a way for you to (solve your problem / make it happen) ". This is for situations where you know they are not satisfied with something or need or want something.

"I think I have found a way for us to improve your cash flow."

"When I thought of people who could make a fortune in a business I found, I thought of you."

Are you still looking for a job (or a different job)? I've found a way for both of us to start a great business without all the risks. "

"Let me ask you a question. If there was a business where you could work part-time from home and that could replace your income with your full-time job, would you be interested?

Examples for unknown market prospects:

"Have you ever thought about diversifying your income?"

"Are you keeping your career options open?"

"Do you plan to do what you do now for the rest of your career?"

You can follow these booklets for the unknown market, or any variation with the following: "I have something that may interest you. Now is not the time to talk about it, but ... ". The Indirect Strategy

This is another powerful tool to help people overcome their initial resistance and thus educate them on what you have to offer. Indirect Strategy is about asking for the help, advice or opinion of a prospect. I used this strategy a lot and it was very useful to me when I first started. Due to my lack of credibility at 23 years of age, I could not be successful with Direct Strategy, so I learned to seek to be calmer while growing the prospect's ego. It worked really well for me and it still works today.

Examples for known market prospects:

"I just started a new business, and I am really nervous. Before starting I need to practice with someone friendly. Would you mind if I practice with you? (This one is GREAT for close family or friends.)

"I found a business that really excites me, but what do I know? You have so much experience. Could you watch it for me and tell me if I'm making the right decision?

"A friend told me that the best thing I could do when starting a business was to have the people I respect take a look at it and offer their advice. Could you do that for me?

Examples for unknown market prospects:

When you meet someone from another city, state, or country, and if the company does business with that region, you can say:

"My company is expanding. Would you do me a favor and check something out and tell me if you think it might work for the region you live in? "

When you meet someone who could give you a great opinion about your product, you can say:

"I have started a business with a product that I think makes a lot of sense, but I would like to hear your opinion. Could you take a look and give me your opinion? "

The Super Indirect Strategy

The third strategy is the Super Indirect Strategy. This strategy is incredibly powerful as it works on a psychological level. In this strategy, you tell the prospect that they are not a prospect and that you only want to know if they know someone who can benefit from your business. It is very effective.

Examples for known market prospects:

"Clearly the business I'm in is not for you, but I wanted to ask if you know someone who has ambition, wants money, and is excited about the idea of having more cash flow in their lives."

"Who do you know that might be looking for a strong business that they can participate in from home?"

"Who do you know who has problems with their business and who is looking for a way to diversify their income?"

"I work with a company that is expanding in your area and I am looking for insightful people who want some extra money. Do you know someone who can fit that description?

In most cases, they will ask you for more information before giving you a name (behind each request there will be curiosity and intrigue, thinking that this could be for them, but they will not admit it yet).

When asked for more information, you can respond with this:

"That makes sense. You want to know more before referring any of your contacts ". So, you can go to step four.

Examples for unknown market prospects:

The unknown market is exactly the same as the known market when it comes to the Super Indirect Strategy. Just use the script for the known market or whatever variation you are comfortable with. Step Four: Yes, do you?

This question has been my secret weapon for a long time. It is the most powerful phrase I have come across and it helps build a great and successful Network Marketing business.

"If I gave you a DVD, would you watch it?"

"If I gave you a CD, would you listen to it?"

"If I gave you a brochure (magazine, or some other printed material), would you read it?"

"If I gave you a link to a website with a full presentation, would you check it out?"

"If I invited you to a webinar that is by special invitation only, would you check it out?"

"If I invited you to a conference call that is by special invitation only, would you do it?"

This question is SO POWERFUL, and for many reasons.

First, is reciprocal. You are saying that you will do something if they do something. As human beings, we are programmed to respond positively to these types of situations.

Second, puts you in a position of power. You are in control. You are not begging. You are not asking for favors. You are only offering an exchange of securities.

86

And third, it implies that YOU have something of value to offer. You are saying that you will do something, but only if the other person does something in return. When you value what you have, people will respect you.

When I started, I did not know about this magical question. He just said things like: "I really, really, really want you to see my video, try my product, listen to this CD, etc." You can imagine the results. The psychology of this is very weak. If you use "If I, will you?", You are having a business conversation. If you use: "Really, truly, I really want you to," now you sound very desperate, and a desperate dealer is NOT attractive. If you have used this strategy, you already know what I am talking about.

"Yes, do you?" gives you results. It makes people say "yes." It helps prospects see what we have in a different way. Remember, our goal is education and understanding. "Yes, do you?" helps you achieve that goal.

If you started the call urgently, praised the prospect, made the invitation, and asked, "Yes, would you?", Their answer will be "yes" almost 100% of the time, and you can go to step five.

If they ask for more information first, just reply with: "I understand you want more information, but everything you are looking for is on the (DVD, CD, printed material, website, etc.). The fastest way for you to really understand what I am saying will be for you to review that material. So, if I gave it to you, would you check it out? "

If they say no, thank them for their time and move on. Also, review steps one through three to see if you could have done better. DO NOT give them your material.

Now you finished the first four steps, and the person said yes! They have agreed to review your tool! Does that mean they will? No. In fact, only 5% of your prospects will do what they said they would if you only used the first four steps

- and 5% is not a good number. To get closer to 80%, you need to complete the invitation process professionally.

Step Five: Confirmation #1 - Time Commitment

You already asked, "If I, will you?", And they have said yes. The next step is to make a time commitment.

"When do you think you will definitely be able to watch the DVD?"

"When do you think you will definitely be able to listen to the CD?"

"When do you think you will definitely be able to read the magazine?" "When do you think you will definitely be able to check the website link?"

Don't suggest them when they can do it (that's another mistake I made when I started in this profession). You just ask the question and wait for them to answer. The question makes them think about their schedule and commitments, find a time to review your tool, and share it with you. In other words, it makes it real.

When you asked "If I, will you?" And they said yes, that means that maybe one day they will. When you get a time commitment, it starts to get real. The only thing that matters is that they tell you when. It doesn't matter what time or date they give you. Let them think about their schedule and tell you when they have definitely reviewed the material.

About 90% of the time, they will give you an answer. The other 10% of the time, they will give a vague answer such as, "I'll try to do it sometime." If they say that to you, answer: "I don't want to waste your time and I don't want to waste mine. Why don't we establish when you can definitely review it? " Remember, they already said during step four that they would review it. You are only confirming when they will.

The key to all of this is that they have already said yes twice - the first time when they answered "Yes, will you?", And the second time when you received a time commitment from them.

So now you can give them the tool, right? No. You're not done yet. Professionals take a few more seconds to complete other steps before finishing.

Step Six: Confirmation # 2 - Confirm the time commitment

If they tell you they will watch the DVD on Tuesday night, your response should be something like, "So if I call you on Wednesday morning, you will have seen it by now, right?" If they say they'll listen to the CD by Thursday morning, your answer should be, "So if I call on Thursday, you've already heard it, right?" If they tell you that they will review the league by July 1, your response should be: "So if I call on July 2, you will have already reviewed it, right?"

They will say yes or adjust the time a bit. In any case, the importance of step six is that they have now confirmed three times already and are more likely to do so - plus:

The key is that this is not a date that you set. It is an appointment that they established.

They said that they would review the material, that they would do it at a specific time and that if you called them later, they would have already reviewed the material. You asked all the questions. Their answers set the date.

Step Seven: Confirmation # 3 - Schedule the next call

This step is easy. Just ask: "What number and what time would it be better to call you?" They will tell you what works best for them, and now if you have a real date. All you have to do is make sure you remember to call them at the time you said you would.

They have said yes four times. The entire invitation took a few minutes and your probability of achieving your education and understanding goal has risen from around 5% to around 80%.

Step Eight: Hang up

Remember, you're in a hurry, right? Once you've confirmed the appointment, the best thing you can say to someone is something like this: "Great, we'll talk later. I have to go!".

Many people manage to make a date and then manage to spoil it by continuing to talk more and more. Remember, our goal is education and understanding and we will let the tool do much of the work. Here are some examples for the eight steps:

A person who hates his job-Direct Strategy

"Hello, I don't have much time to talk, but it was very important to be able to call you. Listen, you are one of the smartest people when it comes to finances that I know, and I have always respected you for that. When you told me you didn't like your job, was it serious or were you just kidding? " (They say it was serious).

"Well, I think I've found a way for you to create an exit option. I have a CD that better describes what I mention to you. If I gave it to you, would you listen to it? (They say yes.)

"When do you think you can definitely hear it? (They say Tuesday). "So if I call on Wednesday, you've already heard, right?" (They say yes).

"Well, I'll call you then. At what number and at what time would it be better to call you? " (They give you the information).

"Perfect. We talk then. I have to go. Thanks!"

A Good Friend-Indirect Strategy

"Hi, I'm on my way out, but I needed to talk to you quickly. You have a second? Cool. You have always supported me and I really appreciate it. "

"I have just started a new business and I am very nervous. But before continuing I need to practice with someone friendly.

94

Would you mind practicing with me? (They say they will).

"Excellent! If I gave you a DVD that presents all the information in a professional way, would you watch it? " (They say yes).

"It lasts about 15 minutes. When do you think you could definitely see it? " (They say Thursday).

"So if I call on Friday morning, you've already checked, right? Excellent. At what number and at what time would it be better to call you? " (They give you the information).

"Perfect. We talk then. I have to go. Thank you!".

A very successful person-Super Indirect Strategy

"I know you are very busy, and I also have a million things to do, but I am glad I found you. You are very successful, and I have always respected you for the way you do your business. "

"I recently started something new and am looking for insightful people. Clearly, this is not for you, but I wanted to ask you if you know someone who is ambitious, who likes money and who is excited about the idea of adding a significant additional flow of money to their lives "(They say they know some people).

"I understand that you want to know more about this before recommending some people. I have a CD that explains exactly what I am doing and what kind of people I am looking for. Is short".

"If I sent it to you, would you review it? (Says they would). "Thanks. When do you think you could definitely see it? " (Says next Monday).

"Well, if I call on Tuesday you will have already checked, right?"

"Well. I call you then. At what number and at what time would it be better to call you? " (They give you the information). "Cool. Thanks again, I really appreciate your help. We will speak on Tuesday".

An unknown market prospect who has done a good job of selling you something - Direct Strategy.

"Now is not the time to talk about this and I have to go, but you are very insightful, and I am looking for people like that. Do you plan to continue doing what you do for the rest of your career? " (They say no).

"Well. I have something that may interest you. Now is not when we should be talking about this, but I have a DVD that explains everything in great detail. If I gave it to you, would you see it? (They say yes). When do you think you could definitely see it? " (They say Sunday).

"Well, if I call on Monday, you've already checked, right?"

(They say yes). "Ok, I'll call you then. At what number and at what time would it be better to call you? " (They give you the information).

"Well, here you go. Thank you for the excellent service, and I will speak with you soon. "

Do you feel how this works? Obviously there are many possible variations for different types of prospects, but I hope these examples help you understand how it all comes together.

When it comes to scripts, it's best if you introduce the basics and don't focus too much on the exact script. Life doesn't work like that. But if you learn to let your prospect know you're in a hurry, praise him, invite him, hand him a tool, ask "Yes, do you?", Confirm using the process outlined above, and finally hang up or complete the invitation, you will do well.

Remember that when recruiting people there are no good or bad experiences - there are only learning experiences. On your way to becoming a Network Marketing professional, the best thing that can happen to you is that you develop the skills to be able to recruit when needed, in any situation. Then you never have to worry about being lucky. So practice, practice, practice.

CHAPTER 6

Skill # 3 — Present Your Product or Opportunity to Your Prospects

We've talked about the first two skills to identify prospects and invite them to learn about your product or opportunity. As you already learned, you will be inviting them to review a tool or attend some kind of event.

If they are going to review a tool for themselves and you won't be there, there is nothing you can do. Only follow up when you said you would. If you are personally there, there are some things you need to understand, and one of the biggest is that ... YOU are not the problem!

This was difficult for me to accept. When I started, I read everything I could, listened to everything I could, and attended every training session that I could. I thought that the most important thing I could do was become an expert on all the data associated with my company because if someone asked me a question, I would have all the answers. Sounds logical right?

I would sit with someone and say, "Let ME tell you all about our products. Let ME tell you all about our company. Let ME tell you all about our compensation plan. Let ME tell you all about our amazing support system. " There are big problems with that strategy if you are looking to build a large and successful organization. For me, the first problem was that no matter how much I learned, there were always questions that perplexed me. And since I presented myself as an expert, if I didn't have the answer, I made the prospect question the entire opportunity.

The second problem was that most of my prospects knew that I was not an expert. So when I went to them and presented myself as an authority on the subject, they knew it wasn't true. It made them skeptical.

The third problem was that, even if I could truly become an expert, the other distributors in my organization did not have the same desire or willingness to learn. As a result, I was the person who gave each presentation. It is not possible to create an organization that can duplicate if you use this strategy and without duplication, Network Marketing is just a job.

In the early days, that was what Network Marketing represented to me - it was a job. My organization was not growing because I had become a problem. But I was determined to change and began to observe and take note of how the most successful distributors carried out their presentations.

The professionals never made them the problem. More than that, they never presented themselves as an expert.

They acted as a consultant connecting the prospect to tools, events, or other distributors to help educate them. If the prospect asked a question, they guided him to the answer, but did not directly give him the answer. This puzzled me until I began to understand duplication. The professionals knew they could sign the person if they amazed them with their knowledge and experience, but they also knew that it would take a long time for their new distributor to do the same, so they found an easier strategy.

It was around this time that I heard a concept that has stuck with me ever since:

In Network Marketing, it doesn't matter what works. Only what is duplicated matters.

This should be a guiding principle for every Network Marketing Professional.

Professionals use tools instead of their own wisdom. Professionals use live events in place of their own presentations. Professionals use other distributors to provide the data rather than provide it themselves. Professionals do not present themselves as professionals, they only invite people to learn about the product or opportunity and allow third-party resources to end up providing the information. Professionals bring with them passion, enthusiasm, excitement and conviction. If you ever observe a professional at work, you will appreciate a fire in them that is contagious. Make sure that passion, enthusiasm, excitement, and conviction are your priority, then professionally invite and let third-party resources do the rest.

In addition to learning how to present your product or opportunity effectively during your personal recruiting efforts, it is also important to learn how to present your opportunity to groups of people.

I've heard him say (and I think it's true): "The person with the marker makes the money." In other words, the person in front of the room giving the presentation usually has an above-average income. When I started out I was terrified of speaking in front of other people but I had ambition and as everyone said this was an important skill, I was determined to master it.

I started by learning how to give a short and effective statement. Learning to tell stories was invaluable in growing my business and has been to date. People don't care how much you know, but they DO want to know your story, as long as you don't bore them to death.

I worked on my story for a while and after changing it once or twice, this is what I got: "Hi! My name is Jack Connor and I am a retired failure. By the time I was 23 years old, I had already had 18 jobs and was beginning to think that my future would not be good. I was embarrassed by my lack of results and was desperately looking for a way to make something of my life. In January 1988, I was introduced to Network Marketing and it was something that changed my life. Instead of being scared of the future, now I'm excited. " (And then I would add whatever was appropriate based on my level of success at the time.)

The theme of my story was "if I could do it, anyone can do it." And it worked. I used it all the time. In hotel meetings, in home meetings, on conference calls - everything.

No matter what your background is, you can create a compelling story. I have found that every good story has four elements:

1.   Your background.

2.   The things you don't like about your background.

3.   How Network Marketing or your company rescued you.

4.   Your results, or how you feel about the future.

Take your time to create your story and start telling it at every opportunity you get.

Then I decided to master the presentation on my company opportunity. Again, the concept of modeling successful people came into play. The highest earning person in my company was extremely powerful and effective.

Also, he gave the exact same presentation every time, word for word. So, I recorded his presentation and handwritten it into a notebook. When I completed that step, I recorded my own voice giving the presentation. I did it word for word. Same story, same jokes - it was all exactly his presentation.

After I finished, I played it ... and it was terrible! My voice had no energy. It was boring. Hated it. So, I recorded over and over and over again until it was acceptable. In the end, I had my presentation on audiotape and listened to it over and over in my car. I'd bet I must have listened to that presentation about 500 times, and by then, I'd already memorized it. He knew her inside and out. I could start from anywhere in the presentation and continue from there.

You won't believe the confidence this gave me. I went from being afraid to give a presentation, to constantly looking for the opportunity to do so! I gave the presentation on conference calls, at home meetings, on joint calls, anywhere I could. I became a constant presenter at our local meetings and continued to move to bigger and better venues, even being asked to speak at company conventions.

For me, the evolution to become a presenter went through several stages:

1.   Learn my story.

2.   Learn the standard presentation on the opportunity.

3.   Learn different presentations on training.

A big turning point as a presenter came in 1993. I was 29 years old and starting to be someone in Network Marketing. I was having a conversation with the CEO of the company and who at the time was the number one distributor of the company. company. I can't remember exactly how we took that topic, but I do remember saying something like this to the CEO:

"Well, he (number one distributor) may be better than me at network marketing, but I'm better than him at speaking."

He had said it as a joke, but the CEO raised his eyebrows and said, "Okay, I'll tell you what we'll do. We have our big convention soon. More than 14,000 people will attend. I will give both of you the same amount of time and we will have a private contest. I will choose a few judges and then we will vote to see who did better. "

Wow! Now he was in a bind! I was not a great leader. It didn't have as great an organization or reputation back then as that distributor. So, I did the only thing I had under control. I started to prepare as if my life depended on my presentation. I chose a topic. I wrote my talk, and I rewrote it over and over again. I investigated. I practiced. I recorded myself giving the speech. I did everything that I could do.

When the day came, I had never felt so nervous in my life. Speaking in front of 14,000 people was like speaking to an ocean. But my preparation served me well. I calmed down, put an end to my insecurity, and gave my talk.

The response was overwhelming! The audience literally went wild. I was a little overwhelmed when I walked off stage as they kept clapping and sat down to listen to the number one dealer speech. He did a good job but I must admit I felt very good when the CEO came to congratulate me on winning our private contest. It was definitely a watershed moment.

That speech was long lost, but a copy has just been found recently.

To summarize this skill set, remember a few important things:

1)   When you're looking for prospects, you are the messenger - not the message.- Get out of the way and use a third-party tool.

2)   Learn to tell your story in a way that makes your prospects curious to hear more.

3)   When it comes to speaking in front of a group of people, preparation is key. When you're ready, it's fun.

CHAPTER 7

Skill # 4 — Follow Up With Your Prospects

In MLM, they say that fortune is in the follow-up. I think it's true, as most MLM people don't follow through, at least not as professionals. You need to understand some important concepts if you are going to master this skill.

Concept # 1 - Following up is doing what you said you would do.

If you say you are going to call at a specific time, do so. The Network Marketing Profession is full of people who get excited one minute and then completely disappear the next. Manage your business with the help of a physical or electronic calendar. Be the person who does what he says he is going to do. People will respect you for it.

I was selling real estate in the year before I started Network Marketing. My father and his partner owned the company. One day I was in the office and a gentleman named Chuck Aycock arrived for a meeting with my father at 10 am It was 9:55 am and my father had not arrived at the office. I welcomed Chuck in and told him that my father would be here soon. As soon as 10 am struck, Chuck got up and said, "It's 10 o'clock. Your father is not here. Tell him to call me if he wants to reschedule our meeting. "

I could not believe it. Had he come to the office only to leave 30 seconds after the meeting time? I said, "Mr.

Aycock, I'm sure he'll be here any minute. It is not necessary for him to leave ".

And then he told me something that I never forgot. He said, "Son, a person is either early or late. He is already late and my time is valuable. Tell him to call me if he wants to reschedule our meeting. " And he left!

My father arrived at 10:10 am expecting to see Chuck. I told him what had happened, and he was just as flabbergasted as I was. My father was not someone who was late. This particular morning, he had only been running a little late. He rescheduled the meeting and I found over the years that my father ALWAYS showed up early to his meetings with Mr. Aycock.

What is the lesson in this story? The lesson for me was that people respect someone who does what they say they are going to do. People also respect those who value their own time. If you say you will follow up at a specific time or in a specific way, do so or reschedule the appointment ahead of time.

Concept # 2 - The only reason to have a presentation is to set up the next presentation

When I started, I ended each presentation by saying, "What do you think?" No one told me that this was the worst thing to do. It seemed like the most natural thing to say to me, but my results were terrible.

I asked one of my first mentors for help and he said:

"Eric, the only reason to have a presentation is to set up the next presentation."

That changed my way of thinking. I thought the reason for having a presentation was for the person to sign! He explained to me that if I ended each presentation by establishing the next, the prospect will eventually be educated about the opportunity and be able to make an informed decision.

The goal in my mind changed from "getting" the prospect on the first presentation to just keeping the process alive by setting up the next presentation, and then the next, and the next, until they made a decision. When I made this small improvement, my results improved dramatically.

We previously talked about how to professionally invite your prospect to review what you have to offer. At the end of that process, we go through several steps to set up the NEXT presentation, which is equivalent to your follow-up call. That was your next date.

When you make that call, you'll ask if they reviewed the material. They will say "No, I didn't", or they will say "Yes, I did." Let's talk about how you will set up the following presentation in both cases.

If they say no, that they did not have time to review the material, it is important that you do not show that you are upset that you did not keep your word. It's funny how many people immediately scold their prospects saying, "I thought you said you probably would have already checked!" Obviously, this will not help you build the good relationship that you are working on.

The best way to respond is: "That's good. I understand that sometimes life occupies us. When do you think you can definitely review it? " Now, you could say that "definitely really" is a bit too much, but I have used it for decades in this follow-up situation and I use it well, functional. In any case, use whatever message you like to set up a new date and follow the same steps to get a commitment. Once you have it, include the date and time of the next call (the next presentation), hang up, and call them when you said you would.

If you call them when you said you would and they haven't reviewed the material yet, just repeat the process. Remember, they are setting the appointment and you are being professional by following up on when you said you would.

If you call your prospect and they say yes, and they have reviewed the material, then you will ask them a few smart questions. First of all, you are NOT going to ask: "What do you think?" This only opens the door to the critical part of the prospect's mind and may raise objections to try to sound smart.

The best follow-up question I've used is this: "What did you like the most?" This question will take you in a very positive direction and give you clues about the prospect's level of interest. If they say "the product" then possibly your next presentation will be related to the product. If they say "financial freedom," then your next presentation will be related to the opportunity presented to them.

Another great question to ask is this: "On a scale of one to 10, with one being zero interest and 10 being ready to go right away, where are you right now?" With this question, any number greater than one is GOOD.

It means that they have something of interest. Most of the time, you will get a five or a six. No matter what number they give you, all you are going to ask them is how you can help them reach a higher number. Normally, that answer will depend on how they answered the question: "What did you like the most?"

If the answer is very positive and the number is considerably high, you can go directly to the process to close the deal (which we will see in the next section). If it's not obvious that you can do it, then just set the following presentation.

They may want to try the product, so help them do that and set a follow-up date - a day and time to call them and see what their experience was like (next presentation). They may want to talk to their spouse, so send them home with material they can share with their spouse and set a date and time for your follow-up (the next presentation). Whatever it is, never finish a presentation without setting up the next one. Never! If you do, it's over.

That is what happened to me in the beginning. It made someone see the opportunity. When they finished, I would say to them: "What do you think?" They usually mutter something like "I'll tell you later," or "I'll tell you later," or "I need to think more about this," or something similar. And poof, they disappeared. So when I tried to call them again, I was bugging them. Everything was very uncomfortable.

Once I switched to never ending a presentation without setting up the next, everything changed for the better. I was being professional. I was in control. The prospect had more respect for me and for the opportunity. All of this happened with this small shift in focus.

Concept # 3 - It takes an average of four to six presentations for one person to be a part of this

When people don't understand that the only reason to give a presentation is to set up the next presentation, they put too much pressure on prospects and themselves. In the "some yes, some no, never mind, next" culture of MLM, people focus on one person only once and if they don't decide to sign up right away, they put them aside and never follow up. In many cases, they take it further by damaging the relationship with the prospect thanks to their attitude.

Professionals understand that it takes an average of four to six presentations for a prospect to decide to be a part of this. Your goal is education and understanding. It is difficult to educate someone with just one presentation. So they take them from presentation to presentation to presentation, knowing that eventually it will all make sense. Through that process, they also build a stronger relationship with the prospect. They strengthen a friendship. That helps build trust, and people enjoy working with the people they like.

Four to five presentations is an average, which means that for every person who joins in the first exhibition, there will be one person who takes more than 10 presentations to be part of it. You can never know. Some of the best people in Network Marketing were prospects for years before finally making the decision to be part of the opportunity.

Always maintain your urgency - but be patient.

Concept # 4 - Condense the presentation for better results

Imposters try to convince someone once and then move on. Amateurs try to convince someone with various introductions as time passes. Professionals condense these presentations in the shortest time possible.

People are busy. They constantly have distractions in their life. When you approach them to review something new, it is important that you keep their interest; the best way to do this is to place the presentations as close together as possible.

If you go slowly, you could start with having them review a video. A few weeks later, you get them to listen in on a conference call. A month later, you get them to attend a webinar. After another month, you invite them to a three-person phone call with you and another dealer. This slow process is difficult because between each presentation they can be distracted by their life. It can be almost like starting over at home.

On the other hand, if you can get them to review a video, be part of a conference call, test the product, attend a webinar, participate in a three-person phone call, then attend a meeting in person (or whatever combination of presentations your company uses), and you do it all in one week, you give them a chance to really think about how this can change their lives.

Questions and Objections

At every step of the recruiting process, you will find questions and objections. This is natural. Often times, your prospect will make them sound smart. You don't want it to seem like it's easy to convince them, so they raise objections to make themselves feel better. How you respond is extremely important. If you act defensive, you will plant a doubt in their minds. If you are offensive, you will scare them.

Remember, our goal is education and understanding. You are not looking to win an argument. Our job is to help the blind to see. When someone raises a negative question or if they offer an objection, all they are doing is helping you identify one of their blind spots. It's good to know what they are so you can help your prospects eliminate them.

I'm going to give you some specific tactics to help you overcome objections, but what I want you to remember and focus on are the concepts. Tactics come and go. Concepts are timeless.

I have found that objections fall into two categories. The first is the prospect's limiting belief in their own abilities. They are not sure that they can be successful. The second is a limiting belief regarding Network Marketing. They are not sure that Network Marketing will help them achieve their goals in life.

124

For both categories, one of the best concepts is empathy - how you relate to people. And the best way to relate to someone is to let them know that you are just like them. You had the same doubts, the same questions, the same fears, and you overcame them. Believe it or not, but your story (and the stories of others) will do more for you to overcome objections than anything else.

There is an old tactic called "Feel / Felt / Found." It works on a concept of empathy. When a prospect offers an objection, you respond with this: "I know how you feel. I felt that way. But this is what I found ". You can use that and be very successful. You can also modify it based on your story and your prospect.

When Prospects Have Limiting Beliefs About Their Abilities

Common objections in this category are:

"I don't have the money," "I don't have the time," "It's not for me," "I'm not a salesperson," "I don't know anyone", or

"I'm too old / too young / I have no experience."

Some people teach sophisticated strategies where they make you look smart, and the prospect look stupid.

"You have no money? Do you have a cable bill? You have a cell phone? Do you ever go out to dinner? You have a lot of money. Come on, wake up! ".

OR,

"You do not have time? How long do you want to have that reality in your life? You have to change if you want your life to change! ".

What do you feel when you read that? How would you feel if someone said that to you? Very bad, right? A better strategy for relating to a person is to tell them your story.

When a person tells me "I don't have the money right now", I answer them: "I had the same challenge. I didn't have enough money to pay my bills, much less to start a new business. But when I thought about it, I realized that if I didn't have enough money to pay the bills now, how was that going to change in the future? He was tired of owing money. He was tired of trying to survive. I wanted more out of life. So, do you know what I did? I found a way, and it was the best decision I ever made. Let me ask you something ... if you really felt that this was the opportunity you need to take control of your financial future, do you think you could find a way to make it happen? "

Nine times out of 10 they will tell you that they could find a way. Again, forget the exact words and focus on the concept. I told them that I was just like them, with the same objection. I was telling them about my pain. And I was telling them that I found a way to solve it. As a result, we developed a bond. We related and understood each other. We were in the same situation with the same hopes and dreams.

And if I didn't have a personal story to match theirs, I was telling someone else's story. There are many stories within our company that can apply to virtually any situation. So when a prospect presents their objection to you, you can say this: "I know what you mean. I have a friend who had the exact same problem. Let me tell you his story. "

Can you see how the approach could work with all objections based on a person's limiting beliefs about themselves and their lives? The concept is simple, it has been tested, and it delivers incredible results.

When Prospects Have Limiting Beliefs About Network Marketing

This category includes:

"Is this MLM?"

"Is this one of those things?"

"Is this a pyramid scheme?"

"I am not interested in MLM."

"I don't want to upset my friends" and "How much are you earning?"

Let's start with one that makes people afraid of our profession - "Is this MLM?", Or variations like "Is this one of those things?", Or "Is this a pyramid scheme?", Or " I am not interested in Marketing.

Multilevel ".

Some people freak out when they hear this question. They say something like this: "Pyramid scheme? Like all the corporations in the world? How the government? How all THAT? ".

Instead of freaking out when talking to your prospects, it's important to understand where this question is coming from. My experience tells me that they usually met someone who joined the profession and was unsuccessful or they have tried it themselves (they usually bought a virtual lottery ticket, as I described earlier, and it didn't work for them). This scenario represents more than 90% of the people who will ask this question. The rest of them have heard of opportunities like this and are skeptical about the get-rich-quick promise.

If they ask this kind of question with some emotion, I know they have been involved at some point, so I say this: "Wait. You have a story. What happened? Were you at any time part of Network Marketing? ". Then you have to let them tell their story. That opens them. They lower their defenses. And that allows you to ask a few questions about their experience.

Let me give you a typical example. I'm going through the invitation process when the prospect says, "Wait, is this MLM?" And he says it with emotion. I reply: "Oh, you have a story. Did you try it at some point? What happened?".

He says, "Yes, I joined a company a few years ago, bought the products and lost my money." Then I answer: "What do you think was the reason why you were not successful?"

He says, "Well, my friend convinced me to try it. I didn't have much time and I thought more people would join right away but they didn't. I think they lost interest. " Then I answer: "Do you think you really tried?"

Answer: "No, not really." I answer: "" Do you think that Network Marketing was the problem? Or maybe it was not the right time? "He says:" It was probably not the right time.

See the dynamics? I've had thousands of conversations like this and they are all a little different, but if you ask them a few questions and are friendly during the process, you have a good chance of helping them get rid of their blind spot and take a look at what you have to do. offer.

Also, you can connect with them by saying that you initially had the same objection and telling them how you got over it. If someone uses the word "pyramid" with me, I always say this: "No. Pyramid schemes are illegal, and I would never be part of anything illegal. "

For people who ask with some emotion, I usually answer with this: "Yes, this is Network Marketing. Do you know anything about that?" Again, I am asking questions and waiting for answers. From those answers, I ask more questions and through the process I can achieve my goal of education and understanding.

"I don't want to upset my friends" is a bit different. Again, I connect with them by telling them my story or someone else's story. And then I ask questions like these: "What makes you think that you will upset your friends?", Or "If you really believed in the product, would you tell your friends about it?", And also "If I could show you how Sharing this product with others without looking or sounding like a sales pitch, would that help you? "

The last category is "How much are YOU making?" If you are already making money, this is an excellent question. If not, your answer depends on how long you have been a part of this profession. If you are new, you can tell them that you are just getting started. If you already have time in this and you have not made a lot of money, you can tell them that you are working part time and that you are very excited about your future. You can also say that you are very excited about your future with this company because you knew that things would not change if you did not do something to change.

The other way to answer is by telling your story and then telling the story of people who are making a lot of money. You can even suggest setting up a phone conversation with these people to make them feel more comfortable about the opportunity.

All this takes practice, but if you can learn the concepts, you will see that it is easy. And the other thing that should encourage you is that you will only have these kinds of objections for the rest of your career. There is nothing new here. What I have mentioned in this section is what you will see. Remember, our goal is education and understanding. This is part of the process that makes that goal a reality.

CHAPTER 8

Skill # 5 — Helping Your Prospects Become Customers or Distributors

This skill is a natural by-product of professionally following up. As we go from presentation to presentation, our goal of education and understanding will be met. But that does not mean that the prospect will look for you and ask you for an order form or a request. It is your job to guide them to a decision.

The key to being successful in this area is a combination of having good posture and asking good questions. Good posture refers to the way you function. Your words and actions will help your prospect feel more confident joining your opportunity, or it may cast doubt on them.

When I first started, my posture was terrible. I was trying to "get" people instead of having the higher goal of education and understanding, and prospects could sense my intentions. I was emotionally very attached to the result. You could even say that he was very needy. Every time it got to this part of the process, I really wanted it. Again, the prospect could feel that I was emotionally tied down and that usually drove them away.

Through the lack of results and without even realizing it, I began to assume that people weren't going to be interested. And that assumption started to creep into everything, which led to an obvious result: the prospect wouldn't join.

Most of the time, I was not properly prepared. He didn't have the applications, the starter material, or whatever it took. Think about the impact this had on my prospects on a subconscious level. It seemed that everything he did projected a lack of belief and professionalism.

Instead of asking questions and listening to their answers, I talked and talked and

136

talked. He was more focused on being interesting than being interested. Prospects don't like that. Nobody likes it.

So again, I followed my pattern of modeling the pros. I watched what the best in the business were doing and started copying them. I interviewed the best to understand what they did differently. And slowly I began to see the errors in my strategy.

First, I saw that the professionals are emotionally detached from the outcome. In other words, your goal is education and understanding as you help the prospect make a decision that would positively impact their lives. They don't act like they need it. They are not trying to "get" anyone. They honestly try to help.

Second, they always assume during their strategy. They assume the person will join in as they strongly believe in the opportunity and how it would benefit the prospect. They are solid like a rock. Many of them are actually surprised when a person decides not to get involved.

Third, it was interesting to learn that they promote themselves in much the same way as they promote the product or opportunity. What this means is that they help the prospect make the decision by saying "You have ME!"

When they promote themselves, it's not something like, "I'm going to do everything I can for you." It's something more like this: "We have a great product and a great opportunity, but I'm going to take this to the top and we can do it together." This gives people the peace of mind that they don't have to learn everything on their own.

Fourth, they are always ready. Forever. They have everything they need to get a person started from the right place.

And fifth, they ask over and over and over and over again and are very good at listening. They act as a consultant by helping a person with a problem. The best consultants around the world have many questions to ask before they can offer a solution.   Network   Marketing

Professionals use questions as their most powerful tool.

As you can imagine, it took me some time to figure out all of this, and that was only half of it. The other part was to have the information and it is another thing that must be put into action. I wasn't as talented as the professionals, but I could model what they did, so I started acting like them.

He acted emotionally detached (at first, he really wasn't); I began to act assuming that people would join (in the beginning, it really wasn't like that); I started telling people "... and you have ME! (although at first that was not a great benefit); he was always ready; I started asking a lot of questions and focused more on being interested than being interesting.

And as he continued, he acted less and believed more and more. The same can happen to you.

Let's talk about the questions. If I were a consultant and your job was to determine if an opportunity was good for your client, what would you do? You would ask questions, right?

As you work to help a prospect make a positive decision about your opportunity, you will do the same. But instead of asking "What do you think?" - which gets you nowhere - learn to ask questions that take you in a positive direction.

"Does it make sense to you?"

"What did you like the most about what you just saw?"

"It's very exciting, right?"

"Can you see how this could be an opportunity for you?"

Of these examples, the one I use the most is "What did you like the most?" The answer to this question is almost always positive and gives you clues about the area in which they have the greatest interest.

Then I usually like to say this: "Let me ask you a question. On a scale of one to 10, with one being zero interest and 10 being ready to go right away, where are you right now? " They will give you a number and it is usually very obvious from their number if they need more information before making a decision or if they are getting close to wanting to start right now.

If you feel like they need more information, just guide them to the next presentation that will help them. But if you feel like they're ready to go, ask four questions. This "Four Question Closing" has given me consistent and strong results over the course of my career. If you learn how to use it, you will be surprised how many people you can help.

Question 1:"Based on what you just saw, if you were to only start part-time with this company, roughly how much would you need to earn per month for it to be worth it?" Instead of asking this question, most distributors say something like this: "Would you like to make $ 10,000 a month?" Do not do that. Instead of presetting what you think they want, just ask how much they need to make it worthwhile and wait for their response.

Question # 2:"About how many hours a week can you use to build that kind of income?" Now you have to think and review your mental calendar to see how much time you can spend to get those amounts of money.

Question # 3:"How many months can you work those hours to be able to develop that type of income?" This question makes them think about their commitment if they want to earn the income mentioned in the answer to question # 1.

Question # 4:"If I could show you a way to develop an income of (your answer to question # 1) a month, working (your answer to question # 2) hours a week over (your answer to question # 3) months, would you? would you be ready to start? Most of the time, you will have a positive response. And when people say "sure, show me how," you can pull out your compensation plan and establish a reasonable plan for them to achieve their goals.

On some very rare occasions, people give you unrealistic numbers. They can say they want $ 10,000 a month working two hours a week for a month. This doesn't happen often, but it does. If you find yourself in this situation, you can act as a consultant and say this: "I'm sorry, but your expectations are very high. You can get $ 10,000 a month but it will take many more hours and many more months than you are willing to commit to. If you are willing to change your expectations, we can talk.

If you don't get a positive answer to all four questions, that's fine. It just means that the prospect needs to have more introductions before they are ready. Set the next one and repeat the process once you're done. This skill takes practice, but it is a skill that will help you for the rest of your career. If you are not tired of many people thinking a lot about it and not acting too much, this will help you.

CHAPTER 9

Skill # 6 — Helping Your New Distributor Get Started

In Network Marketing, people spend a lot of effort and a great deal of time and money getting people to sign and join, but then they waste their investment by letting their distributor learn just how to do everything. Professionals don't do that. They set proper expectations, they help deliver quick results, and then they continue to guide the new distributor through the phases of our profession.

I was initially lucky to have a mentor, Michael Nelson, who was very skilled in guiding new distributors. Michael was not part of my line of support, but it was clear that he was the leader in my city. Furthermore, he had a lot of experience in our profession. So I listened to what he had to say, I watched what he did, and I asked a lot of questions.

Back then, he had a small office near my home and I was always there trying to learn something. Michael was a very successful recruiter. He always brought new people. And besides, Michael's people were doing well in business. That was not happening to me. The few people I recruited did nothing.

As I watched Michael, I realized that every time he signed a new distributor, he set up what he called an "Action Plan Interview." I decided to model what he did. So the next time he met a new dealer, I sat close behind them to take notes on their conversation. I did it several times and was surprised to learn that I was conducting the exact same interview each time. I thought if I could learn that interview process, I would have a chance to get your results. Interview For Action Plan - Part One

He validated his decision to become a distributor. He would say things like, "Congratulations on making the decision. I am proud of you for taking charge of your life. From now on, things are going to be different for you and for your family ". It always took less than five minutes, but by the end of this, any doubts they had about becoming a distributor were gone. They felt very good.

Interview For Action Plan - Part Two

He set his expectations. He knew that most people came into our profession with unrealistic expectations, so he always said the same three things:

"If you are successful in this business, it will be because you create success, not me. And if you fail in this business, it will be because you create the failure, not me. You will be the difference between success or failure. I am here to guide you step by step, but I cannot do it for you. I am here to work with you, but I am not you ".

Wow, this was a radical concept, and so different from the conversations I had when starting out with a new person! I would say things like this: "They pay me depending on what you produce, so essentially I work for you!"

Well, what kind of expectation do you think ESO sets in the mind of a new distributor? I also said something like: "WE are going to build this business together", when that was not true. THEY needed to build a business. I could be a resource, but I couldn't do it for them.

What he would say later was this: "My job is to help you become independent of me as quickly as possible. Do you agree that this is a good goal?

Again, this was radical, but it made sense. Until then, I had a group that was extremely dependent on me. They only did something when I pushed them. But Michael had a group that produced himself without his constant help. He had duplication and freedom.

I do not. This established the relationship so that Michael was the master for his group and not its slave. He could show them the skills and then they could then build on it independently.

The third thing he said was this: "There will be ups and downs as you build your business. There will be good times and bad times. I will know that you are in a bad moment when you are not calling me, when you do not attend meetings, when you do not receive calls, when I start hearing excuses - things like that. When that happens to you, and it happens to everyone, how do you want me to take care of it? Do you want me to leave you alone or do you want me to be more persistent and remind you of why you made this decision in the beginning?

This was brilliant because it is true that everyone has moments when they doubt themselves. He let them know that this was natural and, at the same time, established the relationship so that he could put them back on track when it happened.

What Michael accomplished with these three concepts was so different from what I did by promising everything, that it seemed like night and day. With my strategy, the distributor would do nothing and watch me act. And if I was ever really busy or for some reason, I couldn't help him, I became the easy excuse and the reason things weren't working out. With Michael's strategy, people quickly became independent. He could advise them from time to time, but he did not allow his group to use him as an excuse for their lack of results. While my distributors struggled, yours prospered.

Interview For Action Plan - Part Three

Michael would go through a list to get started, to help the new person have a better chance of being successful. The exact plan would be different for each company, but the concept was to do everything possible to get results quickly.

Here are some examples of what you can include on your list to get started:

1)   Make sure your new dealer has appropriate products. Almost all companies have products that can be used personally by the distributor, so make sure your new person is doing that.

Depending on your company, this may include a monthly commitment. It is very important that people develop an emotional attachment to your products and that only happens if they are using and enjoying them.

the benefits. Also, many companies have products that can be tested or used in demonstrations. In that case, new distributors must be appropriately manned so that they can be properly prepared.

2)   Make sure your new dealer has the proper tools. We've talked about the importance of third-party tools in building a large and successful Network Marketing business. Your new distributor needs to be prepared to help your prospects with the tools that allow you to professionally lead them through the presentation process.

3)   Make sure your new dealer goes online. Show him how to find things on the company website, where the next events will take place, where the webinars

will take place, etc. Remember, our goal is to help you become independent as quickly as possible. This is an important step in making that goal a reality.

4)   Make sure your new distributor understands the basic ins and outs of the compensation plan. At first, they don't need to know the whole plan in detail, but they should at least understand the key points as well as what happens financially as they progress through the first levels.

5)   Make sure your new distributor has a fundamental understanding of how to properly invite prospects, so they understand more about what they have to offer. You can prevent them from running around and talking and talking with little or no positive results, all if you give them a short summary.

how and why a professional invitation process works.

Interview For Action Plan - Part Four

Michael helped the new distributor create an action plan to get through the first few levels and challenged them to do it quickly. He understood, and helped me understand, that it will be a race to help the person get results quickly. If they received positive encouragement, they would continue. And if they didn't receive it, they had a tendency to disappear.

Every company is different, so this action plan will also be different. But think about the simple actions you can get people to take during their first week in order to get the best results.

How can you get your first customer?

How can they get their first dealer?

Can you encourage them to attend their first company event?

What steps can you take to help them get their first commission check?

Success in Network Marketing wasn't a real thing for me until I got my first paycheck. When it came, everything changed for me. I started dreaming of creating a better life for myself and my family. Helping your new person get started quickly is vital.

Interview For Action Plan - Part Five

Michael always ended by setting some specific tasks. One thing I've learned is that new distributors crave directions, and they respond incredibly well to simple tasks. Michael always concluded by setting these tasks as well as a deadline by which they had to be completed. He would tell his new distributor to complete it by a specific date. It is like a presentation during the recruitment process. You go from presentation to presentation, but that doesn't end when they become distributors. Professionals continue to move from exposure to exposure, from task to task.

The purpose of all of this is to help the new distributor get "over the line". When someone starts out, there is always a line between success and failure. On one side of the line, it's easier to quit than to continue. On the other side of the line, it is easier to continue than to quit.

What can help a person pass over the line?

- Sign your first client.

- Sign your first dealer.

- Get your first commission check.

- Attend a large company event.

- Make friends within the organization.

- Proclaim your intentions to the world.

- Get promoted to a new level.

- Be recognized for some achievement.

There are hundreds of other things that can help a person go over the line. As a sponsor, it's your job to help them get over the line and STAY on the line. And the line never really goes away. It is always there and you, as a leader, need to be constantly aware of where your people are on an emotional level. That way you can continue to encourage them to never let go of their dreams.

CHAPTER 10

Skill # 7 — Promote Events

In Network Marketing, meetings make money. It's that simple. Yes, technology can help us connect with more people in ways that are becoming more and more efficient, but nothing replaces face-to-face interaction.

Meeting people one at a time, in small groups, or at local or larger-scale events, will have a huge impact on the long-term success of any Network Marketing organization. But one type of event in particular is the biggest. power, and that's the "destiny" event. It can be an event sponsored by the company or one created by whoever is above you in the chain of command, but a "destination" event is one in which most of the attendees move to a different city, stay in a hotel and participate in conferences and conventions.

Some will try to say that destination events are dead in the new technological world and that people will no longer travel for these encounters. All I can tell you is that these people do not have the highest income in our profession. If you study what successful people do to build their Network Marketing organizations, you will find that virtually every one of them uses destination events as a pillar to sustain their businesses.

There is something magical about stepping out of your daily routine and fully focusing on your dreams. Total immersion, even if it's just for a weekend, is a GOOD thing. You can use it to redirect and re-commit to your future and build up the strength to go home and do whatever it takes to boost your business.

You get strength from the presentations that you have to listen to during the event. Sometimes a person says something at the right time in your life and it changes you forever. More than 20 years ago, I was at a convention when a person named Johnny Daniel said, "You can tell the size of a man by the size of the problem that collapses him." That reflection touched my heart and has helped me ever since. If I ever get sad or depressed, something inside of me says, "Is this Eric's size?" I answer "No", I regain my confidence in myself and I move on.

I've had hundreds of these moments over the years at destination events. I have stopped blaming myself at an event.

I decided to go professional at an event. I realized that no one could stop me at an event. I have decided to reach the top in an event. In fact, when I look back, I can't think of a single significant moment in my Network Marketing career that didn't happen at an event. That's how powerful they are.

In addition to gaining strength from the presenters, you can also receive incredible validation of your decision to get involved. It's a concept called "social proof," and it's extremely important. As human beings, we are programmed to seek evidence from sources outside of our own thoughts and experiences. At destination events, you will meet many other people who have made the same decision that you have made, and that feels good. You will also find those who have overcome their fears and have reached the highest levels of our company.

You will begin to think, "If they can do it, maybe I can too."

There is also a kind of positive pressure from being among your peers. Most destination events include recognition programs - who won the contest, who rose to the next level, who earned the highest income, or who spoke from the stage.

When I participated in my first event and saw all the people walking up and down the stage, I had a thought: "Next time, I'll be walking on that stage." It was inspiring that so many people have achieved what I was yet to achieve. It made me think that I could do it and made me work on a plan to make it possible. Besides being inspired, I didn't want to show up to the next event without any improvement in my business. That positive peer pressure helped me face my fears and make it happen.

In general, the sense of community at destination events is comforting. We all live in a world full of ignorant people when it comes to the Online Marketplace. That can sometimes be daunting. But when we go to a big event, we are surrounded by people who think like US. They have positive beliefs, hopes, dreams, aspirations, and attitudes just like us. Spending time with these fascinating groups of people can fill us up again to have the strength for the next push.

Once you understand how important destination events are to your business success, you need to learn how to effectively promote them for your organization. It's really very simple: The more people in your group attend these events, the more money you will be generating in our profession. Top leaders know exactly how many people are going to attend, and they make sure to increase that number at each new event.

Think about it. Imagine two distributors and each has a group of 100 people. Distributor A makes it a priority and gets everyone to attend top destination events. Dealer B doesn't give it that priority, so only a few attends. Which group will be the most successful? It is not even a competition.

The first step in developing a culture that encourages attendance at destination events is for you personally to be the most committed of all others to attend, and to help others make that same decision. That means you must lead by example, and never miss a destination event.

When I first started in this profession, I did not know how I was going to achieve it. I didn't have the money and couldn't afford the time; he had the same obstacles as anyone else. But something happened to me at my first event that changed everything. I raised enough money to attend, and it was an amazing experience. The stage, the lights, the people, the stories - it was great.

In one of the sessions, I went out to go to the bathroom and when I returned to the entrance of the great convention hall, I was standing next to one of the biggest income generators in the entire company! It was like standing next to a celebrity. He had achieved what I wanted to achieve, and more. I was there trying to think of something smart to say to him. In the end I ended up introducing myself to him and asking him, "What's the secret?"

Today I know that there is no secret and that he could have told me the same thing, but instead he had some compassion on me and gave me a great lesson that has helped me to this day. He said, "Eric, do you see this room? There are around 2,000 people in it. We have these events about 3 times a year. Here is the secret. In the next event, half of these people will not return, but the other half who do return will be earning close to twice the average of the others in that room. Your job is to be within the 1,000 people who return. And it doesn't stop there. In the next event, half of those 1,000 people will not return, but the 500 who return will have income four times the average number of those in the room. This continues from event to event.

I said, "Is that all?" And he replied, "Eric, obviously you are going to have to continue working on your skills between events, but my experience has shown me that if you stay longer than the rest of the people in our great encounters, you will reach the top. " That was something very simple to understand. I thanked him and at that moment I made the commitment not to miss any of the great events of the company.

It was not easy. On some occasions the ticket for the event itself was a problem. I made it a priority and found a way to acquire them. At other times taking care of my children was inconvenient. I searched until I tired of babysitters until we found someone we could trust. Sometimes I had trouble finding a way to get to the event. Instead of taking a nice and comfortable direct flight, I had to book flights with two or three connections. Instead of flying, I sometimes had to drive, even joining a vehicle with a group of people to get there. There were times when I had to book a bus and recruit people from my area to split the costs.

The point is, I made it a priority and came to the event - no excuses or excuses.

When it comes to accommodation, today I stay in suites, but it wasn't always that way. At the beginning it was common for me to share a room with as many people as possible. Instead of ordering room service, we bought groceries from the supermarket to cook inexpensive dishes. The mini bar was religiously out of reach.

The bottom line is that the advice I got so many years ago DOES WORKED. Because I was ambitious and hungry, I found a way to outperform the least engaged people and, as that revenue leader told me, my revenue continued to grow at each event.

Besides that, another strange thing happened. I started to feel different from the others. I started to feel like an "Iron

Man". I began to feel proud of my reality, to continue standing when others had lost faith. So, if you are more committed than the rest to attend destination events, that great commitment to what is important will help you a lot.

Once you are fully committed, the next step is to increase the number of people on your team who attend with you. Most people announce their next big events to their group, they relax and wait for people to sign up. Professionals understand that there is a big difference between being an "advertiser" and being a "promoter".

Promoters make the event a priority for their group. They are tireless with their message. They tell stories that inspire people to act. They take nothing for granted and don't rest until people have signed up. They create a picture in people's minds of how spectacular the event will be and the benefits of attending. One thing that I learned a long time ago was never to take anyone's excuse, at least not at first. I wouldn't finish telling you how many people started giving me their reasons for not being able to attend the next destination event, to realize that their reason was just an excuse, and it wasn't really true.

The problem with amateurs is that they buy the first story they hear and get there. One person says, "I can't quit my job," or, "I can't afford it," or "I can't arrange childcare," or "Who's going to take care of my dog?", Or "I have a birthday party that weekend. " And the amateur says, "Well, that's the way it is. I hope you can attend the next one. "

The professional has his mind programmed in a different way. When they hear an objection, they don't buy that story because they know it's probably not real - or at least not real enough. Instead, they work with that person to help them understand the meaning and importance of attending the event. They then think together with them to find a way to overcome the initial problem.

I can't tell you how many people I've talked to who had already decided not to attend the next event and, in just five minutes, they changed their minds and signed up. The thing to learn from this is that you have to tell your story, not believe theirs.

Think of this skill as if you were a publicly traded company and the value of your shares is tied to how many people you have at each destination event. If that's the case, it would be your priority to ensure that you have a greater number of participants at the next event, right? You can start by attending the first event by yourself, but then the goal should be to bring someone else with you to the next event, and increase that number for the next, and the next, and the next. There is no magic wand in Network Marketing, but this skill is the closest thing to it.

CHAPTER 11

Everything Worth It Takes Time

If a person starts a traditional business, they expect to recoup their investment in the first few years and possibly pay off their initial investment in the first five years. But when a person starts a Network Marketing business, they expect to get their money back in the first month, have returns in the second month, and get rich in the third month. And when that doesn't happen, they end up blaming Network Marketing!

It is as if people do not want the laws of the business world to apply to the Network Market. We DO have a better method, but we are not selling magic beans. Anything worthwhile takes time to develop.

I learned a very important lesson in my early career in Online Market: From time to time throughout your life, your income can take a leap of luck. You may be in the right place at the right time. But if you don't quickly grow as a person to the next level, your income will drop back to the level you really are at. In the end, you only get to do what you are.

How many people do you know who have had a really good time and lost everything? I learned this lesson the hard way in my first months in MLM. It was the year 1988, and I had joined a company that had a $ 5,000 prepayment package, and that paid the sponsor between $ 1,200 and $ 2,400, depending on their level. Even though I am glad that those big money packages have left our profession, back then a person could get big money very fast.

During my first month at that company, I made about $ 7,400! If you remember, my strategy was to call my father's friends before he called them. It was fantastic! In my second month, I made about $ 12,200. Amazing! But that's when the hit of reality hit me. I was not a $ 12,000 a month person. I hadn't worked on my skills. I was not developing. I just let myself go with the flow. My check for the third month was for $ 1,098.60. Seeing that check was seeing myself directly in the mirror. He showed me who he was. It was a horrible feeling.

My first reaction was to give it up and blame everyone and everything for my lousy check. But soon after I realized that in order to earn more, I needed to be more. I needed to work on my skills so I wouldn't have to leave everything to chance, the moment, or my position.

You may have heard, "You can get rich quick," or "You don't have to work," or "The product sells itself," or any kind of overpriced arguments. You must learn to reject those false and unrealistic expectations and work in IT.

Formula 1/3/5/7

There is a formula that I have seen that works in our profession. I call it the formula 1/3/5/7. As a general rule, it will take you a year to be competent and have returns in the Online Market. You will know the basics; you will be able to cover your expenses and you will be learning. It will take you about three years of consistent part-time effort to get to full-time dedication. It will take you about five years of constant effort to have income in the six digits or more. And it will take you about seven years of consistent effort to be an expert.

That doesn't mean you can't do more than that in the short term. Many people do. It just means that if you want to MAINTAIN an income level like that, eventually you need to become an expert.

When you think about it, seven years is not that long, especially when a lot of that is part time. You're going to be seven years older anyway. Anyway, and you could take advantage of being an expert in that period instead of just going with the flow.

How to learn.

Once you make the commitment to focus on your skills, the next step you need to take is to find the best ways to learn. One of the best things that happened to me was realizing that there are no bad experiences or good experiences, only learning experiences. This was a significant discovery. In other words, forget about the result and focus on what you can learn from each experience. This took a lot of pressure off me. I started to focus on HOW MANY experiences I could have, because the more I had, the more I could learn.

Another attribute of being a top earner in MLM is what I call "an active learner." As professionals, they are always learning, they are always growing, and they are always trying to be better. Lou Holtz has said it in the best way: "In this world you are either growing or you are dying, so get active and grow."

I think that is true. Never stop learning.

Model an Attitude of Success.

Try to avoid wanting to reinvent the wheel when you start in this profession. The hard work is already done. No matter what company you are in, it is easy to find someone who is highly successful. It doesn't matter if it's getting customers, finding prospects, inviting, introducing, following up, closing deals, getting people started, organizing an event, or any other skill, right now there are people in your company who have mastered them. And unlike other professions, successful people in your company are willing to share their secrets! All you need to do is model their attitude and you can start enjoying their results. Study

I started with audio programs. In 1988, someone gave me a copy of a talk that J. Rohn had with the Shaklee company, it was called "The Seed and Who the Harvest," and it shook my whole world. I could bet I must have listened to that tape in my car about 500 times. From there, I did my homework on J. Rohn and bought his audio show called "The Challenge to

Success." Mr. Rohn gave me hope, but more than that, he gave me guidance in my continued personal development. The audio program launched my personal development journey.

Through the years, I continued with dozens of different audio shows, all of which helped me incredibly to keep my mind up to date. There is something magical about audio. It whispers in your ear, reminding you of your dreams, your potential, and how to reach them. Also, it is repetitive. You probably won't read a book over and over, but you will listen to an audio program over and over, especially if it's entertaining. And it seems like every time it's different - and it is, because YOU are different.

J. Rohn also taught me to be a reader. No matter what you try to learn, there is someone who has devoted their whole life to that subject and is offering it to you for pennies. Accept that offer.

In our electronic-focused society, and with a lack of attention, it seems that fewer people read books.

That is not true for leaders. More importantly, ask them what they are reading. I wasn't a great reader before joining the Online Marketplace as a professional. But since 1988, I've read an average of four books a month. Those books have shaped my life and my career for the better. Commit to reading only 10 pages a day and in a month, you will be reading a 300 page book. That is a very good start. Video

Videos are also a very good source of learning. Sometimes I like to watch training programs instead of just listening to them. It's part of the reasons I decided to use video as my main focus at NetworkMarketingPro.com. I realized that if I created a short video with interesting information every day, people would receive things of great value.

The Internet has changed the way we learn and obtain information. You can take advantage of online tutorials, watch online videos, attend webinars, or even watch "live" events with streaming technology. Events (edit)

The best way I know to make life-changing information your own is by attending live events. As I've already told you, most of my defining moments have been at events. For one thing, there is always good information for a person who is willing to listen. On the other hand, when you remove all other distractors from your life and just focus, as you do when you are at an event, you have the opportunity to truly listen. Both sides are good.

Beware of Distractors

With all the offerings available in terms of studying your craft now, more than ever, you must be careful about what it is that you allow within your mind. People everywhere will try to distract you with their latest and greatest discovery and it can be very tempting to participate in those opportunities. You should focus on narrowing down your skills: Find prospects, invite, introduce, follow up, close deals, get people started, and promote events.

Make sure you master THOSE skills before adding anything else to your to-do list.

Act

Almost all learning in MLM is in the doing. If you want to learn how to talk to people over the phone, then talk to more people over the phone. If you want to learn how to make presentations at home, then do more presentations at home. You will surely figure out how to do it. That does not mean that you should not continue to seek the knowledge in the skills necessary to be successful in MLM, but it does mean that you should not wait to have all the knowledge before starting to act.

Part of the reason people avoid acting is because they are afraid of making a fool of themselves. If you want to be successful in Network Marketing, you must learn to put fear aside. Here's why: It's very difficult to look good and get better at the same time. Instead of being afraid of how you look when you are learning and growing, be afraid of not acting and living a life at a fraction of your potential.

Let me give you a concept that has served me for more than 20 years in the field of developing my skills. In the early 90's, a friend and I started looking for a great product for Network Marketing. We traveled across the country and met many interesting people. Our journey led us to an organization in Michigan called the High Scope Educational Research Foundation. They have a proven, progressive method of teaching children to learn more effectively.

High Scope has several components, but one that impressed me then and that I have used to this day is called "planbeam-check". The process is explained as follows: "In the plan-have-check process, children make plans, carry them out, and then reflect on what they have done. By doing this, children learn to take initiative, to solve problems, to work with others, and to achieve their goals - this game becomes something with better purpose and focus. By making the plan-do-review process a successful and integral part of students' daily activities, you will learn that you can promote learning and strengthen children's interests and intrinsic motivation. ”

As I listened to what they said about using it as a teaching tool for children, the only thing that was on my mind was how I could use it for myself and for the people in my organization. Even though things didn't work out to turn High Scope into a Network Marketing product, I will always be grateful to you for helping me and hundreds of thousands of people around the world who are using this concept to build better businesses.

Here we will see how I have used and taught the concept for more than 20 years:

Choose a skill that you want to develop.

1.	Make a PLAN.

2.   DO what you planned.

3.   REVIEW your results to see how you can do better next time.

Most people don't make a plan, they just go out.

MAKE. There are still many more people who never REVIEW their results to see how they can improve. Do you see how all of this relates to the fact that there are no good and bad experiences, only learning experiences?

1.   Make a PLAN.

2.   DO what you planned.

3.   REVIEW your results, good or bad, to see how you can do better next time.

4.   Make a better PLAN.

5.   MAKE that best plan.

6.   REVIEW those results, good or bad, to see how you can do better next time.

7.   Never stop applying the plan-do-review process and sooner or later you will become an expert through trial and error.

This little "secret" to learning MLM is one of the most powerful I have ever shared. It has become part of my DNA and I hope the same will happen to you. Teaches

Would you be surprised if you knew that teaching is one of the best ways to learn? It's true. If you really want to master something, teach others. Teaching makes things stick in your brain like no other method.

Nobody but ME! I have to think about it, prepare it and present a message every day, so it helps me to be agile and on top of what I know. The lesson for each of you would be to find someone to teach, even if you only have one person in that group. Start this way as your group grows, look for more and more opportunities to teach. You will be the most benefited. Your relationships

This is another important lesson from Jim Rohn. He taught me the Law of Relationships which says that you will be the average of the five people you spend the most time with. You will think as they think, you will act as they act, you will speak as they speak, and you will earn what they earn. Let me tell you one thing: that law is real. You cannot go against him.

I have done three things throughout my career when it comes to my relationships.

First, I have stopped associating with people who were toxic to my life. This is not an easy decision, but it is a very important one. Some people will constantly have you down.

Second, I have limited my relationships with negative people or with people who were not helping me in my growth towards my dreams. I have learned to spend less time with these people and more time with positive influences.

And third, I have worked to expand my relationships with people who can help me be a better person and a better professional. If you intend to learn to be an expert in the Network Market Profession, it makes sense to find a way to spend more time with people who have the skills you are looking for, right?

If it's a stressful thing for you to think about when you're analyzing the five people, you're currently spending your time with, here's a little tip: About every six months, one of those five people will change. They will move, get a new job, start a relationship, end a relationship - something will happen. The secret is that, when that happens, choose wisely when you are thinking about who is going to occupy that place. Most people will not think about this at all. They only allow the new person to take that place. That's a big mistake. Find someone to push you forward. Find someone who inspires you.

I hope these suggestions on the learning processes to be a professional have been helpful to you.

It's okay to dream big, but you also have to be patient. Anything of value takes time. Continue to develop your skills and become a permanent student. Those skills will be with you for the rest of your life.

There is one more concept that I need you to understand. I've looked at the top earners in Network Marketing, interviewed them, and we've become friends. Do you know what they all have in common? They work hard. Don't get me wrong, they have a high standard of living and love what they do, but they break their souls doing it. If you want to be successful in MLM, you will have to do the same.

In the Network Market it is not about luck, opportunity, location or registering that magical person who will make you rich. Freedom is possible, but it is not free. It will take hard work to be consistent when the world tries to distract you. It will take hard work to learn the skills necessary for long-term success. It will take a lot of effort to be the leader you are meant to be.

Some people in Network Marketing get discouraged when they realize that work is required. Most of them join expecting it to be a vacation. When they feel the pain of growth, they run away. Be different. It can be difficult to work but it is a good job and it is the best way I know for the average person to enjoy full freedom.

CHAPTER 12

Everything is worth it

Network Marketing can be challenging. It is an emotional experience. The ups and downs can be dramatic. But, in the end and for many reasons, it is all worth it. The career that you will create.

If you decide to become a Network Marketing Professional, you will not only create an income for yourself, you will also create a career. I think about this a lot. I consider the skills necessary to be a doctor, a lawyer, the CEO of a large company, or even a world-class musician. We are talking about a high level of skills, and a high level of income.

Now consider the skills needed to become a Network Marketing Professional. They are Tiny in comparison! And yet Network Marketing Professionals have higher levels of income and certainly a greater degree of freedom.

If you take a look at my career, there is a barrier to entry (how hard it is to get in) and a long-term profit (what you get once you get in). For example, a doctor might have 12 years of school plus a medical residency. That requires intelligence that some of us don't have, money that some of us don't have, or even the connections that some of us don't have. In the end, they manage to enjoy a long-term benefit (although many of them would say that such benefit is not worth their investment).

There is always a range between the barrier to entry and long-term profit. There is no question in my mind as to how, of all the professions in the world, the Network Marketing profession ranks the best when compared to the low barrier to entry and high long-term returns on your investment.

One of the best decisions in my life was to pursue a career in Network Marketing instead of just wasting my time. Becoming a professional made a huge difference, and now it's so much fun spending a lot of my time helping other people do the same.

The Freedom You Will Enjoy

Freedom is an interesting word. When it comes to work, I think we understand the concept, but not the full meaning. For me, freedom means having options. It means living the life that I want to live instead of the life that other people want me to live.

Do you remember the imagination you had when you were a child? Imagine your life without limits.

- You wake up when you finish sleeping.

- You do work that is rewarding and makes you happy.

- You can work with people you enjoy.

- You don't have to give in all the time.

• You work when you want to work, but you also play when you want to play.

• You spend a lot of time with people who are important to you.

• You are living large and not wasting your time in a box.

When you have a clear picture of what freedom really is, you will see that the price to pay in Network Marketing is very low. Facing your fears and living a free life is easy. Spending the rest of your days living half your life is a difficult thing.

The Lives You Will Touch

It's one thing to create freedom for yourself and your family, but it's another thing to help someone else do the same.

There are so many people fighting in this world. You have the ability to help people see what they can do for their benefit. You can give hope to those who don't have it. You can encourage them to achieve their dreams. You can give them the inspiration they need to overcome their fears.

One of my greatest joys is appearing in someone else's testimonial. It's great to hear that someone was lost and that somehow, no matter how small, I was able to help them find their way. Network Marketing allows you to do this on a large scale. Not only do you help one person, but you help hundreds or even thousands to live a better life. And the most exciting thing is that this is just the beginning.

It is like throwing a stone into a pond. When it reaches the water you can see the ripples get bigger and bigger until they touch each edge of the pond. In Network Marketing, sometimes you don't see the waves. Maybe you are aware of the impact you had on one person's life, or maybe two or three more waves, but the effect continues to grow regardless of whether you see it or not.

That is why I do what I do. This is why I wrote this book. I know it will have a positive impact on people and that is a stone thrown in the water. But then they will have a positive impact on others and the ripples begin, and then those people will do the same, over and over and over again.

With Network Marketing, you can really make a difference. The People You'll Meet

Network Marketing has introduced me to the most amazing people. This profession gives you an opportunity to not only expand your group of friends, but also to be able to spend more time with them. You will never find a more passionate group of entrepreneurs in any other profession. These people love life and spend their time encouraging each other. Here's an example of what that means to me and what it could mean to you. You can name practically any state in the United States of America or almost any country in the world, and immediately the image of a friend comes to mind.

Network Marketing has also introduced me to many of my heroes. I have been fortunate enough to share the stage and become friends with great people, including A. Robbins, B. Tracy, D. Waitley, the late S. Covey, T. Peters, L. Brown, the late Og Mandino, D. Bach, R. Kiyosaki, H. Mackay, A. Williams, K. Blanchard, T. Rath, D. Pink, M. V. Hansen, J. Canfield, J. Gitomer, G. Vaynerchuk, T. Hopkins, and many, many more. On top of all that, I have been able to learn from more MLM Professionals who have made at least a million dollars than I can count. All of them have had a positive impact on my life and my career.

This profession also helped me get to know my amazing wife, Marina. She was in Moscow for a big MLM training event, and she attended the event with her family. Since she could speak many languages, she was helping translate behind the scenes. I was in love. Our first date was in Red Square at midnight, after the event, with the snow gently falling around us. I will never forget. We have been together ever since. I am not saying that you will find the love of your life in MLM, but I am saying that you will find friendships that will last a lifetime.

The Places You Will See

If you build a large and successful Network Marketing business, a few things will happen. First, you will win some trips that will be the best trips of your life. Second, you will need to support your organization as it expands to all the territories or countries in which the company does business. And third, you will have enough time and money to travel wherever and whenever you want.

It has been said that your life can be measured based on the number and intensity of lived experiences. If that's true, I've already lived a long life. I have visited every state in the United States except Alaska, which will change soon. I have visited more than 40 countries in the world. I have been able to swim in the Great Reef, stroll through Hagia Sofia in Istanbul, visit the twin towers in Malasya, boating around James Bond Island off the coast of Thailand, the tent cities in Nigeria, riding a huge wheel of Fortune at the Port of Singapore, I was on a private tour of the White House, I watched a New

Years sunrise at the Grand Canyon, I enjoyed a 30-course meal at the world famous El Bulli restaurant in Spain, I traveled the canals from Amsterdam,

ALL this and much more has been a reality because I accepted the great profession of Network Marketing. The same can happen to you.

The Causes You Can Contribute To

There are many noble causes. Maybe you want to give some money to your parents or someone in your family, or to an organization that means something to you. In 2011, I asked Harvey Mackay, famous writer, successful businessman, and community activist, about his secret to success. He told me this story.

"Eric, my father sat with me after I graduated from the University of Minnesota at 21 years old. I was a bit arrogant; I was going to make the world my own, I was going to start at the top and go higher and higher. So he said to me, 'Harvey, 25 percent, a quarter of your life, from now on, will be dedicated to volunteering.' I didn't know what he meant, other than that I started volunteering for everything. On the United Way, the Boy Scouts, the Salvation Army, the March of Dimes, everything. Let me tell you what that experience has done for me throughout my life. By being on all those councils and being a part of so many charities, I became a better communicator. I became a better leader. I became a better salesperson because all I was doing was raising money for the 20+ councils I've been to. I became a better sales manager. Can you imagine how many new people I met just from being a volunteer? My network grew enormously.

But the best thing that happened was my sense of being a citizen of the world. Knowing that you managed to help another human being and being able to see the results - it's an incredible feeling. I am very grateful to my father for his advice that changed my life ".

This interview changed MY life as it impacted my way of thinking about contributing. I had always thought that there was only one way to help a noble cause, and that was with your money. But after my conversation with Harvey, I realized that there are three ways to help.

The first is with your money. You can certainly write a check, and that's very good. Network Marketing can allow you to write bigger checks than you ever imagined.

The second is with your time. As Harvey said, you can dedicate a part of your life to causes that are important to you. He chose 25 percent. You can choose what you want, but I advise you to do it. And by time, I don't mean you spend a few hours here and there in a shelter or doing something. I mean spend your time creative thinking, raising awareness, and raising money.

And the third is probably the most important, and that is using your influence. Use the time you will spend supporting your cause and place everything on your influence. Inspire your organization to do something great with you. Encourage your company to get involved. Use your network to do great things. You are powerful and even more so because of your participation in Network Marketing. Use your influences for good. It will change your life and make it better. The Person You Will Become in the Process

Network Marketing changed my life for the better because it forced me to become a better person. As a profession, we bring products and services to customers who want them, but our real purpose runs even deeper.

At its core, this profession is an incubator for personal growth.

- You will learn to face your fears.

- You will learn how to solve problems.

- You will learn how to feed your mind with the positive and protect it from the negative.

- You will learn how to make yourself stronger.

- You will learn how to be a leader.

When I first started in this profession, I did almost everything in fear. He was afraid of not succeeding. I was afraid that my prospects would run out. I was afraid that the opportunity would pass me by. But, with the passage of time, that fear disappeared. I decided to focus on myself and my abilities instead of all the things that I couldn't control, and then everything became clearer. I learned the real secret of Network Marketing.

The greatest benefit is not getting what you want. The biggest benefit is what you will need to become to get what you want. I learned what has always been there, and what has been passed down from generation to generation. The journey is everything.

Thank you for taking this journey with me. Let me conclude by sharing what I say at the end of each Network Marketing Pro video. Ladies and gentlemen, my wish for you is that you decide to become Network Marketing Professionals - that you decide to go Pro, for it is a fact that we have a better way. Now let's tell the world.